# CHOCOLATE
## THE FOOD OF THE GODS

# CHOCOLATE
## THE FOOD OF THE GODS

CHANTAL COADY

*Illustrated by*
# LIZ WRIGHT

CHRONICLE BOOKS

# Dedication

To my mother Sybil, without whom none
of this would have been possible

First published in the United States in 1993 by
CHRONICLE BOOKS

First published in Great Britain in 1993 by
Pavilion Books Limited

Text and recipes copyright © 1993 by Chantal Coady
Illustrations copyright © 1993 by Liz Wright
Designed by Janet James

Library of Congress Cataloging-in-Publication Data

Coady, Chantal.
Chocolate: food of the gods/Chantal Coady: illustrations by Liz
Wright.
p.    cm.
Includes bibliographical references and index.
ISBN 0-8118-0451-8
1. Cookery (Chocolate)   2. Chocolate.    I. Title.
TX767.C5C65    1993
641.3'374 – dc20

92–44428
CIP

Printed in Singapore by Tien Wah


Distributed in Canada by Raincoast Books
112 East Third Ave., Vancouver, B.C. V5T 1C8

10   9   8   7   6   5   4   3   2   1

Chronicle Books
275 Fifth Street
San Francisco, CA 94103

# CONTENTS

CHOCOLATES

CHOCOLATES

# INTRODUCTION

**C**hocolate has always enthralled me. It has loomed large in my life ever since I was a small child of four or five in Addis Ababa. Each Saturday, with my sister and brother, I attended catechism classes there in a spooky crypt where an ancient priest paced the aisles, and afterwards my mother would collect us, proffering Cadbury's Milk Tray bars. However hard I try, I can recall nothing of the doctrine, only the agonizing decisions about which shape to eat first: the lime barrel, the strawberry creme or the hazelnut caramel? Equally popular were the Italian Easter eggs, elaborately wrapped in crisp metallic paper, and each containing a surprise: once the chocolate shell was broken open, a small toy would be revealed. A year or so later we were back in London, where our next-door neighbour was Granny Scala. She was famous for the artificial roses she planted in her garden in the winter, and also for her seemingly endless supplies of threepenny bars of Cadbury's Dairy Milk; long, thin, flat tablets, wrapped in purple foil. Then there was our family doctor, kind grandfatherly Dr Barnes, who always produced a packet of chocolate buttons when we visited his surgery. I'm sure everyone has childhood memories like these.

My passion for chocolate evolved as I grew up, and has now become all-consuming. My professional involvement began almost by chance, when I was a student at Camberwell School of Art. One lunchtime I went to meet a friend, who had a holiday job in the chocolate department in Harrods. As I waited for her, I feasted my eyes on the rows and rows of chocolates, in all shapes and sizes. I was startled out of my reverie by a voice asking me if I was looking for a Saturday job. A childhood dream had come true! Within a couple of weeks, I had undergone staff training, and was dressed in white overalls and gloves, waiting to serve my first customer.

I continued to work there every Saturday until I graduated in Textile Design. Then I had to make a decision about my future career. The textile industry was going through a terrible recession, and I was already fairly disillusioned with what I had learned of it from my time at Art School, so I began contemplating other alternatives. The idea of setting up a chocolate shop started as a joke during an exuberant dinner party, but even in the cold light of the next day I could not stop thinking about it. I was convinced that I could do something much more exciting than anything to be found in England at that time. Also, judging from my experiences in Harrods, there were a lot of chocolate fiends out there waiting for someone like me. Fired with the energy and confidence of youth, I bulldozed ahead and in March 1983, at the age of twenty-three, I opened my chocolate shop, which I named Rococo.

I first heard the word 'rococo' during a radio quiz game, when it was used in a pejorative sense. I was enchanted by the sound of the word and curious as to its meaning. Consulting the dictionary – which said, 'of a style of decoration prevalent in eighteenth-century Europe, with scroll-work, shell motifs, etc.; highly ornamented, florid [almost] to the point of bad taste' – merely confirmed my instinctive interpretation. Later, when it came to the naming of my enterprise, this favourite word seemed a natural choice. It trips off the tongue and suggests a sense of theatre. All the historical references provided an ideal framework for my scheme. In setting up my shop I was inspired to create a fantasy world recalling powdered wigs, pomp and extravagance. I remain convinced that chocolate had its heyday in eighteenth-century London, and I can identify with this period more than any other.

The famous British sweet tooth is probably the result of severe rationing during World War II, or maybe it is because of our nostalgia for all things from the nursery, which appears to have arrested the collective development of the nation. Compared to the rest of Europe, we Britons remain incredibly unsophisticated in our culinary leanings – although we are catching up fast. No doubt the Industrial Revolution also had a profound effect on our food industry: steamed white bread, pressurized beer, battery hens and corned beef are just a few examples of our taste for bland, homogeneous products. Surprisingly, the aims of chocolate manufacturers in Britain were altruistic, and I will expand on this later in the book.

These noble ideals have long since been overlaid with hard business sense. It is sad to think that, as a result of commercial pressures, we are in danger of losing many rare varieties of plant and animal life. This is the consequence of our search for genetically stronger and higher yielding plant varieties. We are already paying the price for past mistakes which affect our health and environment.

The chocolate industry at large is guilty on several counts. The pursuit of mass production has led to the finest criollo beans being replaced by indifferent forastero beans, and expensive pure vanilla by artificial vanillin. More importantly, cocoa butter, the most sensual element in chocolate, is being replaced by solid vegetable oils. The advantages of these oils are that they cost a fraction of the price of cocoa butter, and that they serve to stabilize chocolate, so that it can survive far from ideal storage conditions, and thus lengthen its shelf life. By contrast, cocoa butter literally 'melts in the mouth' at the comparatively low temperature of 34°C (93°F), and it is the crystalline structure of cocoa butter which gives real chocolate its distinctive crisp snap. Also, unlike palm oil and shea nut butter (the two saturated fats most commonly used as cocoa butter substitutes), pure cocoa butter is not easily absorbed, and – according to recent research conducted in France – can actually lower cholesterol levels.

As I have become aware of how greatly chocolate quality can vary, I have begun to feel the importance of raising people's awareness of fine chocolate, just as has been done for wine, cheese, malt whisky and numerous other gourmet delights in recent years. Compared with these, it seemed that chocolate in Britain remained something of a poor relation. I was inspired to put matters to rights, by forming for the first time in Britain a society devoted to fine chocolate. In 1991 The Chocolate Society was launched. I am convinced that we are on the verge of an unprecedented chocolate renaissance which will counter some of the outrageous commercial practices outlined above. I believe that there are many people who have been waiting for such an organization, which will make it easier for them to satisfy their passion for chocolate, without the need to feel bad about eating it.

Chocolate tasting has much in common with wine tasting, as we shall see in Chapter 4. However, whereas wines can survive for decades under perfect conditions, chocolate unfortunately is much less durable. This means that one can only speculate as to the exact flavours of the chocolate consumed in bygone days. Fashions certainly played a part in the flavourings of each era. Many of the seventeenth- and eighteenth-century recipes feature musk, amber and orange-flower water. Amber, now called ambergris, is an oily grey substance found floating on the southern seas, the product of sperm whales. I suspect that these exotic ingredients were favoured almost as much for their rarity value as for their distinctive aromas, and indeed are used only by perfume makers today.

In the course of this book I will be tracing the history of

chocolate through the centuries, from its discovery by Columbus to the present day. We will see how, after being enjoyed for many years by the Spanish court, chocolate drinking spread throughout Europe and eventually back to America and all over the world.

Having been an expensive luxury enjoyed by a few, in the nineteenth century chocolate began to be produced in huge quantities, and I will examine the great family firms which spearheaded the chocolate revolution and the developments that led to the many forms of chocolate that we enjoy today. We shall see how chocolate is made and tasted, and review its many uses: as a medieval medicine, as a religious symbol, as a luxury gift, and as a vital dietary supplement and morale booster for soldiers, sailors and civilians alike. I shall also be discussing the various claims that have been made about the effects it can have on our health.

Finally I will be providing some chocolate recipes, including some very old ones. Among the historical manuscripts, several recipes have come to light, including one for 'Chocolat à l'ancienne' (meaning 'old-style chocolate'), which Mozart tasted at Mannheim.

I hope, in the course of this book, to explode some of the many myths surrounding chocolate so that its delicious taste might be enjoyed to the full and without guilt by those of us who love chocolate at its pure and unadulterated best.

CHAPTER ONE

# AMERICA'S LIQUID TREASURE

**C**hristopher Columbus, like Vasco de Gama, was from Genoa, the prosperous Italian city-state renowned for its trading and seafaring. Both men were in effect maritime mercenaries, engaged in the race to find a new sea passage to the spice islands of the East – all the overland trade routes being blocked by the Mongol hordes. Hoping to obtain funds for his bold expedition across the Atlantic, Columbus approached the kings of Portugal, Spain, France and even despatched his brother Bartholomew to England to ask King Henry VII to invest in the enterprise. Henry, who was much preoccupied with domestic problems following the Wars of the Roses, did not take up the offer, and thus lost a golden opportunity to extend his territories to another continent. He also, indirectly, deprived himself and his subjects of the experience of drinking chocolate, which was not to reach England until the mid-seventeenth century.

In August 1492, having finally persuaded Ferdinand and Isabella of Spain of the potential of his undertaking, Columbus set sail with three small ships and the promise that he would be viceroy of any land he discovered and conquered, and that he would receive a tenth of any gold or silver he found. Setting off

westwards into the unknown, he failed to reach the spice islands of the East (the East Indies), instead making his first landfall in the Caribbean, (hence the name 'West' Indies) on the island of Guanaja in the Bahamas, subsequently on Cuba, and finally on La Isla Española (Hispaniola, shared today by Haiti and the Dominican Republic) where his flagship, the *Santa María*, was wrecked.

The two remaining ships returned to Spain with a negligible amount of gold, no deposits having been found on the islands, but with a group of Carib captives who created a sensation at the Spanish court and provided enormous propaganda value for Columbus and led to a second expedition in 1493 of seventeen ships and fifteen hundred men.

Columbus made four voyages to the new continent and it was on the fourth, in 1502, that he came across cocoa beans, which he presented to the Spanish court. Columbus himself had not enjoyed drinking the spicy, scummy liquid, which contained cocoa, cinnamon, aniseed and cornmeal, and therefore probably was not surprised when Ferdinand and Isabella dismissed chocolate as a bizarre tribal concoction.

The Spanish exploration of the Americas continued, and some twenty years later, when an improved version of the drink was imported to Spain, it was a different story. This time sugar, from the East Indies, and vanilla from Mexico had been mixed with the cocoa, resulting in a more palatable mixture. The court was so taken with chocolate that they kept the secret to themselves for as long as possible. The conquistador Hernán Cortés was the first European to grasp the importance of cocoa, during his encounters with the Aztecs in Mexico, and it was he who successfully introduced the drink to the Spanish court, along with the implements used by the Aztecs to prepare it.

When he left Cuba in 1519, attracted to Mexico by rumours of gold and jewels, the thought of cocoa and chocolate would scarcely have been in his mind. He set sail with a force of five hundred and fifty men, sixteen horses and a few cannon, a tiny army in comparison to the vast numbers of Native Americans he was to meet on the mainland. The fact that in the course of the next two years he was able to conquer the Aztec empire is still a source of amazement to historians. When he first landed his men, horses and firearms, the natives were astonished and frightened, because they had never seen horses or white men, not to mention the destructive ability of the cannon, a demonstration of which Cortés was not slow to perform.

From his capital Tenochtitlán, modern day Mexico City, the Aztec emperor Montezuma sent gifts of silver and gold to the coast in an attempt to persuade the Spaniards to leave. To prevent any of his men from doing so, Cortés burnt his boats, showing intelligence and foresight by burying the metal frames of the boats, which he would later re-use in the final battle, which was fought on the lakes surrounding Tenochtitlán.

Fighting and negotiating with both friendly and hostile Indians, showing cruelty and ruthlessness where necessary, and surviving treachery from all quarters, Cortés headed towards the centre of the country until he finally looked down onto Lake Téxcoco, in the middle of which were the fortifications and temples of the city of Tenochtitlán. Crossing the causeway that led to the city, Cortés was astonished at the welcome he received, having expected to do battle with the people he took to be savages. Montezuma had been closely

following Cortés' progress as he moved inland, and was waiting to receive the man he took to be Quetzalcoatl (the plumed serpent god of Aztec mythology) and his retinue.

Cortés was awe-struck by the scale of his reception, and the pomp and circumstance afforded him. A banquet was prepared in his honour; there were over three hundred dishes, of wild duck, turkey, guinea pig and other exotic birds and beasts. Turkey and guinea pig were native, domesticated animals of the Americas, and until that time unknown in Europe. To drink there were thousands of jugs of *xocolatl*, made from cocoa which was offered to Cortés and his men in sumptuous goblets of pure gold, with golden spoons inlaid with tortoiseshell, examples of the great skill of the Aztec jewellers. Cortés accepted all Montezuma's hospitality, and the soldiers enjoyed the entertainments laid on for them, in the form of juggling dwarfs and dancing girls. After the feast was over, Montezuma is reputed to have retired to his harem, fortified by the aphrodisiac qualities of the *xocolatl*. The troupe of entertainers was rewarded with the remains of the feast, although only the male members would have been allowed to drink the *xocolatl* which was forbidden to Aztec women.

All that Cortés saw would have confirmed that he was at the centre of a highly organized and sophisticated civilization, and indeed the Mayan people had developed mathematical and astronomical systems which had enabled them to calculate a calendar more accurate than our own. Unfortunately, little remains of these records as they were destroyed by the Spaniards. From their worship of the sun gods we do have a tangible legacy in the form of the massive pyramids and the temples they built. There is much evidence too of pottery, sculpture and metal-smelting which survives from the pre-Columbian era. Their writing systems relied on hieroglyphs and the wheel was unknown to them. There have been numerous theories about how they came to be in South America, since so many of their systems and skills parallel other cultures, such as the ancient Egyptians and even the lost tribe of Israel.

One theory is that long before Columbus arrived on the shores of the Americas, others had made the journey. Montezuma is reputed to have told Cortés that his tribe originally came in boats, across the seas, from the east where the sun rises. A more plausible theory is that in 15,000 BC, before the last ice age, there was a bridge of land which enabled the people of Asia to migrate to Alaska. From there they travelled through the Americas. Later the ice melted and the sea levels rose, creating a new continent.

All of the pre-Columbian Native Americans worshipped several gods, and most of them also indulged in the practice of human sacrifice. The Aztec empire was in the grip of a particularly fierce and bloodthirsty religious regime. They believed that without sacrifice, the sun would not rise in the east, the maize on which they depended would not grow, and time itself would stop. To this end there were human sacrifices every day and thousands might be slaughtered on feast days, their still beating hearts removed and offered to the insatiable sun god. By extraordinary coincidence, according to Aztec astrology, 1519 was predicted as the year when a white-faced king named Quetzalcoatl would return to release the people from this horrific need to appease the gods. The Aztec legend began in the ninth century AD, when there had been a king called Quetzalcoatl. He was a great poet and philosopher, and had the divine power to breathe life into inanimate objects just by looking at them. His other identity was the plumed serpent god (in Aztec culture there was no difference between being a king or a god). Quetzalcoatl became disenchanted with the practice of human sacrifice, and after a time declared that he was going to go far away, to the lands across the seas, towards the rising sun. He promised to return, in another time, and another guise, and told them to be prepared for the event. This was the main reason why Cortés' small force had been able to penetrate so deeply into the heart of the empire, and with so little opposition. It was not long however before Montezuma realized that he had made a serious mistake.

Despite the friendliness and extravagance of his welcome, Cortés' position was obviously highly insecure at the centre of this vast empire, where he and his men were little more than special food for the gods. Realizing this, he kidnapped Montezuma, and during the course of the next two years dealt not only with the hostile local Indians but also with a force sent by the Spanish Governor of Cuba, who was worried that Cortés had become too powerful. Cortés quickly won the soldiers round to his cause and they became reinforcements to his small army. Then with boats built from the skeletons of the ones he had already burnt, Cortés embarked on his final assault and destruction of the Aztec capital. In August 1521 the remains of Tenochtitlán became the capital of New Spain.

How was it possible for such a small force of Spaniards to break up the great Aztec Empire in such a short space of time? The Europeans certainly enjoyed better military technology, together with their horses and firearms. Also, soon after landing on the mainland in Tabasco state, Cortés was given an Aztec Indian girl named Marina by some friendly natives. She understood both the Aztec language and Mayan, and was to become a faithful mistress, invaluable ally, interpreter and

adviser during the conquest. Doubtless it was partly with her help that Cortés won the collaboration of various native tribes in the course of his campaigns. These tribes had long been subjugated by the Aztecs, and were more than willing to hasten the end of a bloodthirsty regime. Cortés' own powers as a leader and soldier were undoubtedly supreme. Another factor was smallpox which spread like wildfire in the Indian population who had no immunity to this and other newly imported diseases. But perhaps most important of all was the inherent weakness of a system which was haunted by the possibility of complete and sudden cataclysm, in the form of the sun failing to rise. The arrival of Cortés and the events of 1519 to 1521 proved to be equally catastrophic.

Although gold and silver may have been Cortés' main priority, he did not quickly forget the *xocolatl* that had been consumed at that memorable feast. The name *xocolatl* meant bitter water (xoc = bitter; atle = water). There is also a theory that the word *xoc* or *choc* comes from the sound of the chocolate being milled by the wooden stick called a *molinillo*, which makes a 'choc-choc' noise. Certainly their brew was very different from the drinking chocolate which we know today. It was essentially a cold, savoury drink, with chillies, cinnamon and cloves. The addition of cornmeal served to absorb the fat (cocoa butter) which floated to the top, and acted as a crude emulsifier, binding the fat and the water. It is difficult to imagine anything further from the unctuous hot melted chocolate drinks which one can find in such modern shrines as 'La Maison de Chocolat' in Paris! There is also evidence from early Spanish accounts that the Aztecs had blocks of cacao ready prepared in order to facilitate the speedy production of thousands of jugs of *xocolatl*.

Cortés had also observed that cocoa was used by the Aztecs as a form of currency. A fellow countryman, Hernando de Oviedo Valdez, reported that he had bought a slave for 100 cocoa nibs (a nib is an almond-sized cocoa bean). A rabbit could be exchanged for 4 nibs, the favours of a woman of the

night for 10 nibs, and so on. The Aztecs had imposed a feudal system on their subjugated tribes, which required all taxes to be paid in the form of cocoa beans. This may have given Cortés the idea that it was possible to grow money on trees, and so he started to cultivate cocoa on a large scale. All the cocoa that the Aztecs drank, and used as money, was grown by the Mayan people on the Yucatán Peninsula, where the warm, humid climatic conditions were ideal. The Mayans had been cultivating cocoa for at least six hundred years after migrating there in AD 600. By AD 1200, with their own civilization in decline, they had become subjects of the Aztec Empire.

On his travels Cortés established cocoa plantations all around the Caribbean from Mexico to Trinidad and Haiti, and also to Fernando Po, which is off the coast of West Africa. It was from Fernando Po that a blacksmith named Tette Quesi is reputed to have returned to his native Gold Coast in 1879 with some cocoa seeds in his pocket, and started the first cocoa plantation in Africa.

During the sixteenth century, Spanish colonization spread to South America. In Venezuela it resulted in the severe depletion of the Indian population. Around 1600, with the introduction of cocoa cultivation, the structure of the Venezuelan economy was established for the next three hundred years. As cultivation spread out from Caracas and the central coastal valleys, cattle raising was pushed southward from the highlands into the northern parts of the Llanos. In the Caracas of 1684 wealth was amazingly concentrated: 172 people held a total of 167 cocoa plantations with 450,000 trees. By the 1740s, cocoa production in the province of Caracas had multiplied tenfold, but the number of cocoa proprietors had increased by only three. The domination of the land by a single commercial crop continued until the end of the eighteenth century. The colonists dispossessed the small indigenous producers. The church controlled about a fifth of the cocoa area in the 1740s, but even this was less than the area owned by a single family, the Pontes.

Venezuelan production seems large until compared with that of the much smaller area of the French colony of Saint Domingue, present-day Haiti, which in fact produced ten times as much cocoa. The reasons for the relative inefficiency in Venezuela included higher taxes and absentee landowners who left production in the hands of dishonest and inefficient administrators, but the main difficulty was the lack of a reliable labour supply. The remaining natives preferred to practise subsistence farming in family units rather than hire themselves out as labour. To remedy this deficiency, African slaves were imported, but because the slaves tended to have few children and were also able to buy back their freedom, the labour problem remained.

Peruvian cocoa was inferior to Venezuelan, but that exported through Guayaquil, the principal port in Peru, was also cheaper. Exports totalled 11,310 tons in 1820. From the beginning, cocoa was exported to Spain and Mexico. Contraband trade also reached Curaçao, which was occupied by the Dutch in 1634. By the end of the eighteenth century wars were disrupting shipping. Since cocoa beans deteriorate rapidly when stored in humid conditions, their cultivation was gradually replaced by more stable products such as coffee, cotton and indigo.

In Brazil, as in Venezuela, the principal problem of cultivation was a shortage of labour. The Portuguese had passed laws against taking native slaves early in the eighteenth century. (It is ironic that 150 years later the Portuguese were the main protagonists of slave labour in Africa – see the Cadbury trial in Chapter 3.) It was very much in the economic interests of the colonial settlers to violate these laws. This led to a struggle with the Jesuit missionaries. The Jesuits were expelled from the main cities on two occasions, and in the 1720s a campaign of complaints against them contributed to their ultimate expulsion from Brazil.

Between 1678 and 1681, the Portuguese crown tried without success to stimulate cocoa production by offering tax exemptions to producers. The colonists preferred to send their Native American guides after the wild cocoa of the Amazon forest rather than cultivate the sweeter domestic kind. Little capital was needed to gather wild cocoa. Slowly the market for Amazonian cocoa developed in Spain and Italy, and the trade increased. In the mid-1720s about 100 licences were granted for canoes going to gather cocoa. By the 1730s this figure had risen to 250, and by 1736 it stood at 320.

Before 1755 cocoa was the major export of Para (the centre of Brazil's cocoa-growing areas). It commanded high prices on the Lisbon market. Thereafter, exports became more irregular because of labour and shipping shortages and a drop in cocoa prices. However, we need to remember that from the natives' perspective the issue was not one of labour but of survival. The demands made by the Portuguese and the mistreatment they meted out took their toll. In addition, epidemic diseases decimated the native population. There were smallpox epidemics in 1621 and 1644, and a devastating measles epidemic in the 1740s. Each outbreak was followed by a shortage of labour that led to renewed introduction of slaves.

In Mexico, meanwhile, there were large numbers of Spaniards living in established colonies, with their wives and families, who behaved as if they were still in Spain. The upper-class ladies of Chiapas had chocolate brought into the

cathedral by their maids. The following famous tale was told in 1625 by Thomas Gage, an English Catholic friar, who had been educated in Xeres, Spain, by the Dominican Friars. (He was smuggled to New Spain in a biscuit barrel – because only Spaniards were allowed to visit their new territories.) In a story of 'death by chocolate', Gage tells of expatriate Spanish gentlewomen who claimed that they could not endure the long daily masses in the cathedral in Chiapas without refreshment. Each instructed her maid to come with a jug of chocolate, disrupting the ceremony so much that the Bishop decreed an excommunication order on anyone partaking of chocolate within the cathedral walls. Soon after this he was mysteriously poisoned by a cup of chocolate, and died after a week of agony. Nonetheless he is reported to have said prayers during his last hours for those who had caused his death. Gage, who lived in Chiapas in New Spain for fourteen years, was the first to record the use of chocolate as a gift. When he left Chiapas the Governor's wife gave him many boxes of aromatical (ready spiced) chocolate. Travelling missionaries were often given boxes of chocolate. The nuns of Oaxaca were famed for their chocolate, which was sent to other parts of Mexico and to Spain, and it was the nuns of Puebla who created the dish of Mole Poblano (turkey in chocolate and chilli sauce) in honour of a visiting archbishop.

Another local custom was to use the drink *xocolatl* as wages for the Native American guides who travelled with the missionaries. Thomas Gage was advised to keep to this custom and not to set a precedent by offering money. Also, whenever the natives co-operated to build or repair each other's houses, they rewarded their helpful friends with 'great cups of chocolate as big as will hold a pint'. This peasant version of the drink did not include the costly ingredients used by the Spaniards, just a little aniseed and chilli for flavouring.

Chocolate had been used as a form of taxation in Montezuma's reign. The Spanish priests continued this tradition by imposing unofficial taxation on the natives, in the form of more or less compulsory offerings. Gifts of chocolate, honey, chickens, maize and candles were required to be offered to the priests on feast days, and during Lent.

CHOCOLATE

## EARLY CHOCOLATE MANUFACTURE

The first detailed account of the preparation of the drink comes from the Italian merchant seaman Benzoni in 1540. On his travels in the New World, he came across Native Americans preparing cocoa. He was intrigued by the sight of the drink, but was not tempted to try it until his supply of wine had been used up. He watched them drying the cocoa beans, roasting them in earthen pans over a fire, and grinding them between the stones which they also used to grind flour for their bread. They put the resulting paste in cups of calabash, a kind of gourd, and mixed it with water. They then used a special wooden stick, called a *molinillo*, to beat the mixture. Maize was added as a primitive emulsifier, to help incorporate the cocoa butter. (It was not until the nineteenth century that a Dutch chemist called Van Houten finally worked out how to extract the cocoa butter, to produce the dry cocoa powder which we know today.) Benzoni found the drink bitter, yet satisfying: refreshing without being intoxicating. He also notes its sustaining properties, and the fact that the Native Americans who drank it regularly had thought him foolish to have been so disdainful at first of their nourishing drink.

Thomas Gage also details the usage of chocolate, and its preparation into blocks in the 16th and early 17th Centuries. The paste would be formed into square or round shapes, which were carried in boxes. This proved to be a convenient form to keep it in before the final preparation into a drink, and must be the first method of manufacture of cocoa. It was drunk widely in Mexico, and regarded as the best of drinks, though its value as money must have limited the amount consumed by the poor.

In the mid-seventeenth century the basic Mexican recipe adopted throughout Europe for the preparation of drinking chocolate was cocoa beans, sugar, cinnamon, red pepper, cloves, logwood (similar to fennel) and aniseed. Other ingredients might also be added. Maize was commonly used, while some people put in almonds and orange-flower water.

The use of maize can already be seen as a double-edged sword: it was helpful in absorbing surplus cocoa butter, but was soon being used excessively to adulterate the drink and thus increase profits. Spaniards sometimes added powdered roses of Alexandria. Antonio Colmenero, a Spanish physician, mentions the first chocolate bars in 1631:

> *Sometimes they make tablets of the sugar and chocolate together . . . and they are sold in the shops, and are confected and eaten together like other sweetmeats.*

These bars would have been in a very crude form; the cocoa would have been roasted and ground, and then, while still warm, shaped into blocks or sticks. These artisan-produced lumps of chocolate can still be found in Mexico and the Caribbean today. The usual way to make a drink, however, was by dissolving the chocolate paste in water, then adding more water with sugar and boiling it, and finally whipping it with a *molinillo*. The resulting oily scum or froth was much appreciated, but not by all. In 1640 the English herbalist John Parkinson referred to chocolate as 'a wash fitter for hogs'.

# CHAPTER TWO

# EUROPE HAS
# A TASTE FOR IT

**B**y the beginning of the seventeenth century, all the trade routes had been well established and documented and maps drawn up. Information about the trade winds and other navigational systems were available to sailors. Exporting cocoa beans to Europe became an important trade. Providing they were carefully stowed, the dry beans were able to withstand the long sea voyage. Antonio Carletti, an Italian, took cocoa to Italy in 1606, after his travels in South America, and from there the news about cocoa travelled swiftly into Germany and Austria. At that time chocolate was enjoyed almost exclusively in liquid form, but it was not like the sweet drink of today. Milk was not added to it. Rather it was strongly concentrated with the addition of hot peppers and spices. Cocoa was still a very expensive commodity, and would only have been served in the most aristocratic circles in Europe.

At this time, a considerable amount of chocolate paste was also being exported from the Spanish New World colonies to Spain and Flanders. Not only had it reached Italy, it was also being introduced into south-western France at about this time by Spanish monks and friars. There, however, it appears to have been confined to the monasteries.

We know that by 1631 chocolate was well established in Spain, Italy and Flanders, especially at court, and was already regarded as a wholesome drink. In 1615, Anne of Austria, daughter of Philip III of Spain, had married Louis XIII of France. She would probably have taken with her to France the century-old Spanish chocolate drinking custom. If not, it certainly arrived there in 1660, when a similar dynastic marriage renewed the Franco-Spanish alliance. This was the marriage of Maria Theresa to Louis XIV. She indeed brought her own personal maid from Spain to make chocolate in the Queen's apartments. The French court nicknamed this maid 'La Molina', after the chocolate-beating stick used at that time. La Molina's tasks were later vividly portrayed by Despina in Mozart's *Cosi fan tutti*:

> *What an abominable life a lady's maid leads!* . . .
> *I've been beating chocolate for half an hour, now*
> *it's ready, and is it my lot to stand and smell it with a*
> *dry mouth?*

Mozart's opera was written a century later, but the custom of private preparation of chocolate drinks in high-born ladies' apartments still persisted. Since the Queen took her chocolate in her private apartments, the fashion did not immediately extend to the French court. Perhaps it was considered a coarse Spanish drink. Yet the drink could not be kept under wraps for long, and within a few years it became a well-established and highly-regarded drink, to be consumed in public.

Maria Theresa is said to have declared: 'Chocolate and the King are my only passions.' You will note that chocolate comes before the King! This may have been a necessary reversal of the usual order of priorities, as the King gave her little of his attention in the early days of their marriage. His main preoccupation was with gaining territories, by diplomacy or war, his ambition being to extend the 'natural boundaries' of France and gain glory and lasting fame. He took his role as head of state very seriously, and was determined, once he was no longer a minor, not to be a puppet. He resolved to be his own chief minister, and worked long hours. In his leisure time he preferred the company of his mistresses.

It was perhaps just as well that the Queen had the consolation of hot chocolate. She was not the last person to use chocolate to assuage life's disappointments. Furthermore, she even succeeded in winning the King over to chocolate. It was served to his guests on reception days, three times a week, though this practice ended in November 1693 for reasons of economy. When the King was succeeded in 1715 by his five-year-old great-grandson, Louis XV, France was ruled by a regent, the Duke of Orleans. The Duke did not have morning receptions (levées), but took chocolate himself in a large room. Those who were allowed in to greet him referred to it as 'being admitted to the Chocolate'. At the same time in Martinique (one of the French colonies), chocolate was used to show the passage of time, or the time of day, in expressions such as: 'I left at the brandy and arrived at the chocolate.' What a life!

From the court in Versailles the use of chocolate had spread to Paris, and as early as 1687 a Parisian directory noted the names and addresses of three chocolate makers, of whom the most famous was David Chaliou. A chocolate maker in those

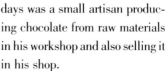

days was a small artisan producing chocolate from raw materials in his workshop and also selling it in his shop.

The production of cups and pots designed especially for chocolate shows just how popular chocolate was becoming in France. Some were made of precious metals, a good example being a silver chocolate set, decorated with golden flowers, which was presented to the Dauphin by the Siamese Ambassador. This thoughtful gift suggests that chocolate was already known, or at any rate that the custom was understood, in the Orient. In 1689 a newspaper reported that the Queen Mother won silver and earthenware chocolate pots and three chocolate batons (used to stir the chocolate) in a lottery organized by the Duke of Orleans at St Cloud. By 1692 wine merchants were complaining that chocolate, coffee and tea were adversely affecting their trade. No doubt these complaints were wildly exaggerated, but it does show that this new drink had made a significant impact on the national awareness.

By 1690 chocolate had arrived in Hanover, and in 1711, the Holy Roman Emperor Charles VI transferred his court, and with it chocolate, from Madrid to Vienna. The chocolate makers of Florence and Venice were already famous. Vienna was to share their renown as it became famous for its delicious cups of chocolate served with glasses of ice cold water, as well as, later, the most famous of all chocolate cakes: the Sacher Hotel's speciality known as *Sachertorte*.

The first printed evidence we have of chocolate being used in London is the notice in the *Public Advertiser* in 1657:

> *In Bishopsgate St is an excellent West India drink called chocolate to be sold, where you may have it ready at any time, and also unmade at reasonable rates.*

By the end of the Commonwealth in 1659, Thomas Rugge, a London diarist, was writing in his Journal about coffee, chocolate and tea as new drinks in London, and referring to chocolate as 'a harty drink in every street'. Chocolate seems to have spread rapidly in London during Charles II's reign. The King's own physician, Henry Stubbe, was a chocolate enthusiast and in 1662 wrote a book in its praise called *The Indian Nectar*. His book confirms that chocolate had by this time spread from Spain and Portugal to Italy, France, Germany and England, and even to Turkey and Persia. Stubbe also tells us that there were two qualities of chocolate – ordinary and royal. The royal variety which the King enjoyed was rich in cocoa, and not too sugary. So we see that the recent demand for chocolate with a high cocoa content has been an issue as far back as the seventeenth century.

## EARLY PRODUCTION METHODS

In the seventeenth century, most cakes of chocolate contained a small proportion of the cocoa nib, but consisted mainly of sugar and other spices. They were coarse, and were to remain so until the nineteenth-century invention of the cocoa press by Van Houten. The fact that there are differences in the quality of the beans had been noted early in chocolate's history. For the King's chocolate, Stubbe chose beans from Caracas and Nicaragua. He also said that, to make excellent chocolate, care was needed at each stage in the processing. The beans must be carefully sweated on mats, fermented and cured. The level of roasting must be carefully supervised; in fact, very little has changed in these two areas. By the 1660s the Spanish court had abandoned the use of five-star anise, nutmeg and maize. Stubbe followed this practice, so the basic chocolate ingredients of the Spanish and English courts were not dissimilar to the cocoa of today, although the drink would still have been a very fatty one.

The seventeenth-century method of manufacture was very much a cottage industry. The cocoa 'nuts' were dried either in a digesting furnace or in a kettle over a fire. This was done gently, stirring and turning carefully, because chocolate becomes bitter if burnt. The nuts were peeled, beaten to a powder and then browned over the fire, as was the spice in a separate process. The hulls were beaten separately and added to the ordinary chocolate, but left out of the best. Finally the spices and cocoa were mixed together and ground further, with a little gentle heat underneath the stone grinding-table. Some makers used iron tables, but they heated too quickly and were much more difficult to control than stone ones. There were many small manufacturers, each doing his own thing, which meant that there were great variations in recipe, method and final product. Needless to say, the huge-scale industry of today produces a much more uniform and predictable product.

The way that a cup of chocolate was made during the seventeenth century varied in the different countries of Europe. In Spain, 1oz of chocolate, 2oz of sugar and 8oz of water were heated and whipped to a froth. In France, the drink was made with either water alone or half milk, half water. English chocolate-houses made it with milk or with egg (sometimes yolk, sometimes white). Coffee-houses too sold chocolate at twopence a dish. Chocolate sweetmeats were made of chocolate, orange-flower water, sugar, ambergris, white of egg and gum dragant (or gum tragacanth, more commonly known as gum Arabic).

The earliest cookbook giving a general recipe including chocolate was published in 1691. Massialot, a seventeenth-century French writer, in his *Royal and Bourgeois Cooking*, included an Aztec recipe for widgeon (wild duck), using chocolate to thicken the sauce.

## CHOCOLATE IN ENGLISH SOCIETY

By the 1660s the drinking of chocolate had been taken up by many 'top' people in England. Samuel Pepys entered in his diary on 24 April 1661 that in order to allay his appalling hangover, following the festivities surrounding the coronation of Charles II, he drank chocolate as a morning-after cure:

> *Waked in the morning with my head in a sad taking*
> *through the last night's drink, which I am very sorry*
> *for; so rose, and went with Mr Creed to drink our*
> *morning draught, which he did give me in Chocolate*
> *to settle my stomach.*

In 1666, when Lady Fanshawe, widow of Charles II's ambassador to Spain, returned to present her accounts to the King, she brought with her: 'ambar skins, gloves, Chocolaty and a great picture by Tishines [Titian].'

Hans Sloane, Physician to Queen Anne and Samuel Pepys, valued chocolate highly for its restorative qualities, and was the first person to try mixing it with milk. This was a closely guarded secret remedy, which was sold to an apothecary after some years. The secret was eventually bought by Cadbury Brothers in 1824, who successfully mass-marketed it. Hans Sloane had already made himself a considerable fortune, and invested some of it in cocoa plantations in Jamaica, where he had first observed the dramatic effects of cocoa in reviving sickly babies.

By 1675 chocolate-houses in London had become centres for gambling, so the King made a Royal Decree to suppress these institutions. In 1702 only five chocolate-houses remained in London: The Chocolate House on Blackheath; The Cocoa Tree, Pall Mall; Lindhearts, King Street, Bloomsbury; The Spread Eagle, Bridge Street, Covent Garden; and Whites, St James Street. However, this does not necessarily indicate a decline in the drinking of chocolate. It was sold at the majority of coffee-houses for twelve pence a quart, or twopence a dish, a price just about double that of coffee or tea. The chocolate- and coffee-houses soon became political clubs, to such an extent that members of opposing parties would be denied entrance. The Cocoa Tree and Ozinda's became the meeting-places for the High Tories. Those who were discontented with the Hanoverians could drink a furtive toast there to the Pretender, James Edward Stuart, known to them as King James III. The leading Whigs met at the St James Coffee House, which became an exclusive social club, and was frequented by the writer Steele and the actor David Garrick.

White's Chocolate House became the meeting-place for the most fashionable men and women. Horace Walpole wrote to Horace Mann on 26 March 1784: 'To the present drama elections I shall shut my ears . . . and when I went to White's preferred a conversation on Newmarket to one on elections.' The main pastimes at White's were gambling and gossip. Even so, the decorous atmosphere of the club was usually maintained, while men lost at cards what they had gained in business. George Harley Drummond, of the famous banking house of Charing Cross, lost £20,000 at whist, and was forced to resign his partnership in the firm. Sir John Malcolm, after losing the fortune he had acquired in India, remarked nonchalantly, 'Another sitting of this kind will oblige me to return again to India.' Women also played and lost. Some went away to borrow more money, and returned to play again, hoping to recoup their losses.

The importance of the coffee-house in London life is shown in the account of a visitor:

> *We rise by nine and those that frequent great men's levees find entertainment at them until eleven, or as in Holland go to tea-tables. About twelve the beau-monde assembles in several chocolate and coffee houses . . . If it be fine weather we take a turn in the park 'till two, when we go to dinner; and if it be dirty; you are entertained at Picket or Basset [a card game resembling Faro] at White's, or you may talk politics at the Smyrna and St James.*

## CHOCOLATE AND TAXATION

During the eighteenth century there was a great increase in the use of chocolate throughout Europe and it was not long before cocoa suffered the same fate as tea and coffee and had duties imposed on it. In 1704 Frederick I of Prussia levied a chocolate tax on every purchase, while in England the early use of cocoa was restricted to the wealthiest echelons of society by punitive taxation. By 1800 this had reached the level of almost two shillings a pound on cocoa imported from British colonies, while foreign cocoa had three times as much duty levied on it. All chocolate – at this stage it was still only drinking chocolate – had to be wrapped in stamped papers, supplied by the excise men, and then sealed proving that the taxes had been paid.

Wherever such fiscal policy exists it is likely to lead to smuggling, counterfeiting and fraud. As far back as the sixteenth century, there are reports of Native Americans filling hollowed out cocoa beans with dirt, keeping the precious nibs for themselves. In the seventeenth century, adulterated chocolate was widespread, the cocoa mixed with such unsavoury additives as starch, shells, and brick dust. This penny pinching continues to this day with many 'chocolate' bars containing as little as 15 per cent cocoa solids. In eighteenth-century England, there were fierce penalties for smuggling or trading in chocolate without a licence, including a £500 fine and a year in prison for knowingly selling chocolate on which the duties had not been paid.

With such levels of taxation and with complex regulations controlling trade, it is a tribute to the seductive qualities of chocolate that it continued to be sold at all in the early 1800s. However, by 1852, duties had plummeted to one penny per pound on colonial cocoa. Quaker industrialist claims of cocoa's health-giving properties, and soaring imports, were two reasons behind the reduction in taxation, and hereafter consumption escalated. Cocoa was now affordable by every

working man, and was vigorously promoted as such by the Quakers. In 1822 a mere 230 tons were imported into Britain, whereas by 1850 this figure had reached 1,400 tons. By 1900 the figure exceeded 12,000 tons.

In England, chocolate was a major feature of the daily life of the eighteenth-century smart set. Addison tells us in the *Spectator* that its use was deemed a token of elegant and fashionable taste. Aristocrats had chocolate prepared for them in their homes by their servants. It was especially popular at breakfast time, as shown by the *Spectator* of 11 March 1712, which quotes a lady's diary:

> *Wednesday. From eight to ten. Drank two dishes of chocolate in bed, and fell asleep after them.*

It was served in elegant porcelain cups with two handles, a saucer and a lid called the cover, and sometimes the sets included matching chocolate pots.

Some fine examples of eighteenth-century china made for the service of chocolate are preserved in London's Victoria and Albert Museum. They are made of porcelain by the Worcester, Chelsea, Derby, Meissen and Schreiber potteries. In earlier times, domestic utensils were mostly of pewter and earthenware, and were seldom decorated. The fastest growth area of porcelain was in the equipment for the new hot drinks of tea, coffee and chocolate. Previously drinks had always been served cold: water, ale and mead were the most common beverages. To a twentieth-century observer it is a little difficult to comprehend that the novelty of chocolate was not simply its taste, but that it was also served hot. At that time earthenware cost about twopence a piece, china about sixpence, so most plates were made of earthenware.

Horace Walpole gave a set of porcelain chocolate cups to his friend Horace Mann, the British representative in Florence. Mann in his thank-you letter remarked that the set was so beautiful that 'it is the ornament of the red room and would be looked at only, except on a grand visit.' This does not imply, however, that the set was seldom used, for Mann was visited by many princes, lords and ladies who much enjoyed drinking chocolate. Walpole also tells us that a party of half a dozen ladies was known as a 'ciocolata'.

Chocolate was already well established as a gift among Europe's renowned and elegant, and was commonly taken by travellers, both for their own use and as a gift. The Empress Elizabeth, widow of Charles VI, gave two parcels of chocolate to Count Bernie, one for his journey to Italy and one to give to Madame de Craon. When the Duke of York, brother of King George III, travelled through Italy in 1764, several cities presented him with gifts of fruit and chocolate. Travel had become a fashionable pastime among the aristocracy. Another fashionable pursuit was the acquisition of ancient Roman and Greek marbles, and other artifacts. The two things seemed to go well together. By now roads were much better than in the seventeenth century – and so was the design of coaches.

Nonetheless, courage was needed to undertake these long slow journeys which, including lengthy stops, lasted for months. The upper classes braved the many hazards, but liked to ensure some modicum of comfort. They carried with them all the necessary equipment for making chocolate. Their children were encouraged to travel, as it was the custom to finish their education by doing the Grand Tour. Horace Walpole was one such young man, and in 1739 he took his chocolate with him, carefully packed away in his luggage, as chocolate was liable to be seized by the French customs.

In 1797 Goethe, the German poet and philosopher, made sure he had his chocolate equipment when travelling in Switzerland. From our current perspective it seems odd that a German should have felt it necessary to take his chocolate with him to Switzerland. However, the Swiss did not actually start manufacturing chocolate until as late as 1845. Rudolph Sprungli-Ammann was the first in the Swiss marketplace, and was so successful that in 1899 he bought out his competitor Lindt, the inventor of the conching machine, for a million-and-a-half golden francs.

## A WIDER DISTRIBUTION

Although the chocolate trade developed throughout the eighteenth century, it is clear from old shop cards, as well as housekeeping accounts kept by customers, that in England not all chocolate was sold by specialists. The Russells of Bloomsbury bought their chocolate not from a chocolate maker but from a grocer who supplied them with many other products. Likewise the Purefoys, a landed Buckinghamshire family, used an agent who bought their chocolate from a grocer called Moulson. Such families living on country estates produced many of their own basic wants, but ordered luxuries such as chocolate, tea and sugar from London grocers. They employed agents who organized the purchasing and transport of such items. Mrs Purefoy, a very determined lady, kept a close eye on these transactions. On one occasion she wrote that the chocolate was so bitter and highly dried that she could not drink it. Perhaps the grocer had heated it too long or too quickly. This complaint also illustrates the variations in quality which one might expect from such small workshops.

Another grocer who supplied chocolate was a woman, Teresa Mocenni of Siena. She was both friend and supplier of the Countess of Albany (Bonnie Prince Charlie's widow) when she lived in Florence. Letters written by the Countess echo this awareness of variations in recipe and quality of chocolate. On 28 November 1797 she wrote saying that the chocolate was good, but she preferred more vanilla. On 25 July 1798 she said the chocolate would be as good as Livornese if it were worked a little more, and smoother. And again on 25 April 1801 she asked for chocolate pastilles, saying, 'Put in as much Vanilla as you can. I would prefer to have the best chocolate even if it is dear.'

In England, chocolate was a very rare luxury for middle-class people. A lawyer called Burrell, living on the then large income of £300 a year, kept a diary between 1691 and 1711, in which he mentions the new hot chocolate drink twice only, once as a gift and once when he drank chocolate in London. The account books of Sarah Fell, of Swarthmoor Hall, include this entry: '1 penny was spent on chocoleta, in November 1675.' She was married to George Fox, founder of the Society of Friends. This may well be the earliest-known reference to a Quaker in connection with chocolate.

Middle-class people living in the country relied on travelling tradesmen for goods not produced locally. For example, the Reverend William Cole was visited from time to time by the Cartwright brothers, who were lace buyers visiting their workers. On one occasion in the Bletchley Diaries, Cole records that they brought him 2lbs of chocolate. It is not clear whether this was as a gift or in exchange for some other service. Clearly some middle-class families did obtain chocolate, but the supply was infrequent and not to be relied upon.

One young lady, Miss Elizabeth Cartwright, who lived on the edge of Nottingham, wrote teasing letters to her good friend Mr Dodsley. He had failed to arrive on two occasions when she had awaited him:

> . . . the Chocolate ready, the Balm Tea prepar'd, my cap put on much tighter than usual; all this done two mornings together, yet no Mr. Dodsley appeared.

The accounts of Abraham Dent, who kept a grocers, mercers and stationers shop in Kirkby Stephen, indicate that chocolate usage in the north of England in the eighteenth century was minimal. Between 1762 and 1765 tea appears often, coffee rarely, and cocoa only once.

So in the course of the three hundred years that had passed since Columbus brought the first cocoa beans back from the New World, the drink of chocolate had slowly evolved into the most appreciated drink of the royal and aristocratic classes throughout Europe. This eminence was already being challenged by coffee and tea, but chocolate, first as a drink and later to eat, was to spread throughout the world, and is still one of the best-loved indulgences today. Its use, even at the end of the eighteenth century, was still confined almost exclusively to the rich and aristocratic, however, and can therefore be compared to the drinking of champagne in our times. The middle and lower classes would have to wait until the nineteenth and twentieth centuries, when reductions in taxation, large-scale manufacturing and improvements in processing and transport would finally enable them too to take part in the great chocolate adventure.

# CHAPTER THREE

# THE CHOCOLATE EXPLOSION

**T**he eighteenth century is often referred to as 'the Age of Enlightenment', and certainly it was a time of enormous change in terms of culture, industry, and mobility. In England, as elsewhere, many great inventors were experimenting with new ideas, and one of them was Walter Churchman. In 1728, Churchman invented an engine for grinding cocoa, powered by the water-wheel. In 1729, he was granted a patent by King George II. He established a factory in Bristol, using his new invention, and took advantage of his proximity to the port, where frequent shipments of cocoa beans from the West Indies arrived. It was at about this time that the 'slave triangle' began. Glass beads and similar merchandise were exported from Bristol to West Africa, where they were traded for slaves. From Africa, slaves were taken to the West Indies and sold. The triangle was completed with a cargo of hardwoods, sugar and cocoa being shipped back to Bristol, and from there distributed around the country by horse-drawn coaches.

In 1765 James Watt perfected Newcomen's steam engine, an event which heralded the Industrial Revolution. Almost overnight, production methods changed from small artisan

workshops to huge mechanized factories. The industries which changed the most were weaving and spinning, but food production was also revolutionized. Chocolate, in particular, was being transformed by the Quakers into a cheap and universal drink that everyone could enjoy. Imports of raw cocoa begin to rise steeply; in 1830, of the 400 tons of raw cocoa cleared through the British customs houses, 260 tons (more than half of all the cocoa imported) were allocated to His Majesty's Navy, and the remaining 140 tons were reserved for domestic consumption.

The idea of serving cocoa to British sailors was introduced as early as 1780 by Captain James Ferguson, who had enjoyed drinking cocoa while the fleet was anchored in Antigua, in the British West Indies. He and the ship's surgeon understood the nutritional value of cocoa, and as a dried provision, it was ideally suited for long sea voyages. Limes provided essential vitamin C, thereby preventing scurvy, while cocoa provided the whole gamut of other vitamins and minerals, as well as valuable and nourishing proteins and fats. The comfort and

stimulation afforded by the drink to men taking the night watch must have been considerable. So by 1824, the cocoa issue, or CI, was instituted in the Navy, and each man received his daily ration (a one-ounce block of chocolate), along with his rum and limes. 'Kye' was the word commonly used by sailors when talking of cocoa, which may have been a derivative form of CI, or perhaps slang for char, or chai, which came from the Indian word for tea, used widely in the British Army.

## THE QUAKERS

At this time the Quakers began to be involved in the cocoa industry. The Society of Friends, better known as the Quakers, was founded in England by George Fox (1624–1691), its aims being to promote justice, equality, forgiveness and under-standing. Fox felt that the established church did little to help the poor, and abused its position of power, by maintaining that the only way to reach God was to be a member of the church. The Quakers challenged this view, asserting that ministers were not essential and that there was something of God in every man, and equally in every woman. Quaker women played a very important role in both the business and the family, and were far more emancipated than their non-Quaker contemporaries.

The Quakers suffered persecution, even imprisonment, on account of their beliefs, which alienated them from almost every branch of the Establishment. They were barred from Oxford and Cambridge Universities because they were dissenters, and also from professions such as politics, law and medicine. Consequently many Quakers seem to have found a natural outlet for their energies in the fields of business and commerce. Several great Quaker families – the Frys, the Rowntrees, the Cadburys and the Terrys – chose cocoa as a commodity because they believed it to be a nourishing drink and a healthy alternative to Dutch gin. They hoped to persuade the poor to give up alcohol, in favour of this altogether healthier drink, and to spend their limited resources on clothes, food and housing, to create a better living environment for themselves. It would be true to say that we owe a great debt to the Quakers for extending the use of cocoa, from being restricted to the rich and aristocratic, to being a food of the people. They promoted the drink as a healthy, 'flesh forming' substance, and created model working environments

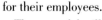

for their employees.

These model villages are still going strong, providing housing for workers and retired employees in Cadbury's Bournville outside Birmingham, Rowntree in York and Hersheyville, Pennsylvania. As a result of the persecution of the sect in England, large numbers of Quakers left for America, and settled in the area west of New York. A colony was founded in 1682 by William Penn. The colony of Pennsylvania later became the second state of the USA. By 1864, some seven thousand Quakers had settled in Pennsylvania, where Milton Hershey

 set up his chocolate factory and model village in 1900.

Joseph Fry (1728–1787) was a Quaker who came to Bristol in 1748, aged twenty, and was later made a freeman of the city. He was an apothecary, who became a chocolate manufacturer, his interest in cocoa stemming from the belief that it was of great medicinal and nutritional value. He was assisted in his enterprise by the use of Walter Churchman's cocoa-grinding engine, having bought the patent from Churchman's son Charles. After Joseph Fry's death, his wife Anna and their son Joseph Storrs Fry I (1767–1835) continued the business. Anna Fry took an active role in it, and after her death her son took on a partner, a certain Mr Hunt, who continued until his retirement in 1822. J. S. Fry I, in his turn, took his sons into the business, forming the now famous J. S. Fry and Sons.

Elizabeth Fry (another member of the famous Fry family) was a Quaker minister, and so was able to visit prisons, which became a focus for her reforming zeal, so appalling were the conditions she witnessed. Another well-established York-based Quaker family were the Tukes, who were also chocolate makers and later linked by marriage to the Rowntree family. William Tuke was horrified when he visited a lunatic asylum in 1791, with a group from the Society of Friends, for at this time it was normal for inmates to be chained up and treated like animals. Within four years he had opened an establishment for the mentally ill, with a care system based on rehabilitation and enlightenment.

The legacy of the Quaker work ethic continues to some extent to this day in Cadburys and Rowntrees, although the working practices are now becoming similar to any other multinational employer. In the early days, there were strict rules governing the segregation of the sexes (only relaxed in the 1950s), compulsory daily readings from the Bible, and free education and healthcare for all the workers and their families.

Through marriage into the Tuke family, Henry Isaac Rowntree took over the business from old William Tuke. This is how Tuke formally announced the change:

> *We have to inform you that we have relinquished the manufacture of cocoa, chocolate and chicory in favour of our friend H I Rowntree, who has been for some time practically engaged in the concern, and whose knowledge of the business and its several departments enables us with confidence to recommend him to the notice of our connection.*
>
> *We remain very respectfully,    Tuke and Company,*
> *York, 1st of seventh month, 1862*

It seems that the Rowntrees were dogged by financial troubles, and also had a policy which forbade advertising. At this time, both Cadburys and Frys were using the new technology invented in 1828 by the Dutchman Coenraad Van Houten, which pressed the cocoa butter from the cocoa liquor. This invention revolutionized the production of cocoa, which until that time had always suffered from the problem of excess fat. As far back as the Aztecs, there is evidence of maize or cornmeal being added to cocoa to absorb the oily residues.

Cadbury and Fry were quick to capitalize on this new selling-point, informing their customers that they were selling the pure, unadulterated extract of cocoa, or cocoa essence, to make drinking chocolate. This was indeed a revolution in the world of cocoa, as it was the first time that a product had been marketed which would dissolve readily in milk or water. Eating chocolate, however, was still some years away.

Rowntrees, unable to make the necessary capital investment to introduce Van Houten's cocoa press, tried to make the best of a bad job by promoting existing lines. Henry Isaac was a light-hearted, witty young man, perhaps the only Rowntree with a bubbling sense of humour. When he took over the business, he gave his products exotic names such as Iceland Moss Cocoa, Hexagon Cocoa, Pearl Cocoa, as well as Flake Cocoa, Farinaceous Cocoa and Tuke's Superior Rock Cocoa –

names that must represent the many different ways in which cocoa was blended with other products to make it more palatable. When Tuke's Superior Rock Cocoa won a local prize, Henry Isaac renamed it Rowntree's Prize Medal Rock Cocoa, and liked to quote a verse from Deuteronomy in its praise: 'For their Rock is not our Rock, even our enemies themselves being judges.'

It seems rather sad and misguided that they were drawing attention to the fact that their products were positively pre-Columbian compared to their rivals, simply because they could not afford a cocoa press. However they did eventually hit upon a money-making formula with their now famous fruit gums, and their fortunes improved. Their other commercial success story is the Kit-Kat snack bar, which has been a market leader since it was introduced in 1933.

The Cadbury family was another of the great Quaker families, starting out as grocers in Birmingham in 1824, and opening their first factory in 1847. The village of Bournville

was created by the Cadbury brothers as a model village with 24 houses for their key employees in 1879. The reasons why Birmingham was chosen initially, were to do with freedom of speech, movement and trade, which were paramount to Quaker ideals.

At Bournville, the Cadbury brothers saw their dream of creating a harmonious environment for their work-force becoming a reality: the land they bought was undeveloped, and left lots of room for future expansion. There was fresh air, a good supply of clean water, and a canal and rail infrastructure in place to make distribution simple and efficient. Today there is a chocolate theme park called 'Cadbury World' on the site, as well as the original village which remains almost unchanged from the early days. The houses are in the contemporary style of the garden suburbs such as Welwyn Garden City, spaciously designed with gardens at the front and back, and in a landscaped environment. To this day their tenants have to meet rigorous standards in maintaining the fabric of the buildings and in renewing the paintwork. Even the length of the grass on their lawns is specified.

The Cadburys were not satisfied with just providing model working environments for all their employees. With the vast profits which were now rolling on, they started to dabble in the world of newspapers, which gave them an ideal platform from which to air their views. In 1906 they even went so far as to sponsor an exhibition at the Queen's Hall, Birmingham, in order to expose the exploitation which so many labourers faced, and thus the National Anti-Sweating League was founded. Its principle aims were to press for a minimum wage, and to improve working conditions, and Mr George Cadbury himself became the League's president.

The factory at Bournville had indeed set new standards in the environment provided for the working man and woman. However, there were certain observers who could not reconcile the Cadburys' proselytizing, paternalistic position with the fact that they were buying slave-grown cocoa. The Cadburys had spoken at length to H. W. Nevinson, author of the book *A Modern Slavery* written in 1906, detailing the horrific conditions of the '*servicaes*'. Cadburys, however, still continued to source their raw materials from these plantations.

The Cadbury brothers soon found themselves in a compromising position, because at this time the conditions of

the cocoa growers in Africa were being widely reported in the press. It was a well-established fact that the Cadburys had been making millions of pounds' profit out of slave-grown cocoa. Labourers were press-ganged, and forced to work in such hot and wet conditions that the average life expectancy on such plantations was about one year. All slaves were issued with a standard five-year contract, and any who miraculously survived the course were automatically issued with another when the first had expired. It was unheard-of for a slave to return home alive.

In 1908 an article was published in the *Standard* by a journalist called H. A. Gwynne. He wrote a piece parodying the model village and factory at Bournville, where the young men and women worked in calm surroundings, and were encouraged to take part in recreational exercises. There was a swimming pool, built especially for them, though in this as well as in the factory, the sexes were strictly segregated (a legacy which continued into the 1950s). Here indeed was ammunition for Gwynne's piece:

> *The white hands of the Bournville chocolate makers are helped by other unseen hands some thousands of miles away, black and brown hands, toiling in plantations, or hauling loads through swamp and forest.*

There was little choice for the Cadburys but to issue a libel action against the *Standard*, which led to a highly publicized trial. After hearing all the evidence, which went on for several days, the jury returned in less than an hour. Cadburys had won the libel case, but little else, for the award was derisory: one farthing, plus costs. It was a salutary experience, and one which forced the Cadburys to look at and improve the conditions on the plantations. Eventually a new system of 'share cropping' on the Gold Coast evolved, which allowed each man to own his plot of land and cultivate the cocoa himself, selling his crop to a co-operative.

Not everyone in the chocolate industry came from quite such high-principled backgrounds as the Quakers. In England there are also two long-established shops, whose histories, if not the chocolates themselves, have a hint of eccentricity. The first is Charbonnel et Walker. The legend is that a French paramour of one of the British royal family was pensioned off in 1875 and, with the proceeds of her alliance, opened a chocolate shop with a certain Mr Walker in Bond Street, London. It exists to this day, and in truly lavish style will keep a record of regular customers' favourite chocolate selections on a card, so that one can simply phone and say, 'A 3lb box of the usual please, my driver will be round in half an hour. . . .'

The other shop is Bendicks, which was the result of a partnership between a Colonel Bendicks and a Mr Dickson, and was founded in 1921 in Mayfair, London. Their most famous, and decidedly English gentleman's club-style chocolate, is the Bendicks Bittermint. Made using a mint fondant centre dipped in unsweetened chocolate, it remains an enduring classic to this day.

## CHOCOLATE ARRIVES IN AMERICA

Considering that America was the home of the cocoa bean, chocolate arrived relatively late in the American Colonies, in about 1755. In 1765, Dr James Baker and John Hannon set up a chocolate factory on the banks of the River Neponset in Massachusetts, which in 1780 became the Walter Baker Company (Walter was James's grandson). It is claimed that this was the first chocolate factory in the United States. The name Baker's is synonymous with quality in the United States, as they produce a range of chocolate bars from the unsweetened to semi-sweet to German-style sweet dark dessert chocolate (it is called Baker's German Sweet Chocolate).

One of the most colourful stories in the history of the American chocolate industry is that of the Ghirardelli Chocolate Company. It had its origins in a company founded in 1849 in San Francisco by an Italian confectioner named Domenico Ghirardelli, who had been attracted to California by

the Gold Rush. He followed the hordes of prospectors into the Sierra foothills, selling them general goods, including coffee and chocolate, from a tent in Stockton. He also opened a confectionery store in the then booming port of San Francisco, but it was destroyed by the great fire of 1851. His Stockton premises also burnt down. Business continued under a succession of different names, but by 1856 it was known as 'Ghirardelli's California Chocolate Manufactory'. Ten years later it was importing 1,000 pounds (half a ton) of cocoa beans a year. By 1885 the overall total had risen to an astonishing 450,000 pounds (200 tons). When Domenico Ghirardelli died in 1894, the business was already in the hands of his sons. From 1900 onwards they specialized in chocolate and mustard, and the company continued to grow and flourish, in buildings that became a famous San Francisco landmark, now known as Ghirardelli Square. It was eventually bought by the Golden Grain Macaroni Company in 1963, and moved to San Leandro in 1967, but Ghirardelli Chocolate continues to be one of the great names of the industry.

## A REVOLUTIONARY INVENTION

The most important invention relating to chocolate production, mentioned earlier, was the cocoa press invented by the Dutch chemist Coenraad Van Houten and used in England, France and Switzerland. By turning a large wooden screw, it pressed the cocoa butter out of the chocolate liquor. The result was a dry, virtually fat-free cocoa powder. Van Houten was granted a patent for his cocoa butter extracting press by Wilhelm I on 4 April 1828, and so established Holland as the leading choco-late-producing country in Europe. He had also developed a system, which has since been called 'Dutching', involving an ancient technique used by the Aztecs: potash was mixed with the cocoa beans in order to darken the colour, lighten the flavour, and create a cocoa powder which dissolves readily

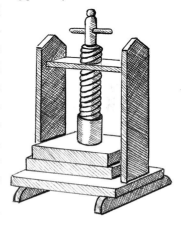

in milk or water. The debate about whether 'Dutching' improves the flavour of cocoa continues to rage, although at the time of this invention in 1825, the English felt that the cocoa butter was an important factor in the nutritional and health-giving properties of cocoa. However, soon both the Frys and the Cadburys had bought machines from Van Houten, and were selling pure cocoa extract. The new trend was for cocoa extract, and it was marketed for its purity and solubility by Cadbury and Fry.

Many people claimed to have been the first to have had the idea of recombining the cocoa butter with the cocoa mass to invent today's chocolate bar. Perhaps, spurred on by Van Houten's new technology, several cocoa manufacturers hit on the idea simultaneously. At any rate in 1842, French Eating Chocolate appeared on Cadburys' price list for the first time, priced at two shillings a bar. John Cadbury stated that all the products were manufactured by themselves in Birmingham.

The first people to experiment with solid bars of milk chocolate were undoubtedly the Swiss partners, Daniel Peter and Henri Nestlé, at Vevey in 1876. The legend is that Henri Nestlé was trying to find a way of condensing milk to mix with his own brand of children's breakfast cereal. Daniel Peter then hit upon the idea of combining this new form of milk with cocoa, cocoa butter and sugar to create milk chocolate, which was marketed under the name 'Peter's'.

In 1892, to celebrate the four-hundredth anniversary of Columbus arriving in America, there was a huge exhibition in Chicago: 'The World's Columbus Exposition.' One of the many visitors was Milton Hershey, a caramel manufacturer from Pennsylvania. He was deeply impressed by a display of German machinery for making chocolate which had been brought over by J. M. Lehmann. Inspired by the sight, and being the classic American entrepreneur, as well as a Quaker, he decided that the caramels which had made him a fortune over the past few years were just a fad, and that chocolate was a really enduring product. It was his ambition to become a pioneer in this new market.

By 1900 Milton Hershey had sold his caramel factory for one million dollars. With the proceeds he built the village of Hersheyville (modelled on the English Quaker examples) near Pennsylvania, and a factory to produce chocolate bars, a product which he firmly believed to be the snack food of the future. His vision and the business have stood the test of time, and much of his fortune has been dedicated to improving the lot of the working classes.

Hershey introduced a milk chocolate bar with almonds. Now everyone was experimenting with new fillings, and moulded shapes, and chocolate technology was progressing in leaps and bounds, as the ever-expanding market-place demanded. Always keen to be in the vanguard of the chocolate industry, Hershey was the first person to experiment with the

use of solid vegetable fats as a substitute for cocoa butter. His objective was to produce a chocolate which would not melt in tropical heat, and in 1911, using his new technology, Hershey introduced a six-ounce bar, which would soon be issued as standard rations to the troops going to war.

During World War II in Great Britain, each civilian was issued with ration books, allowing two ounces of confectionery (to include chocolate) per head per week. This figure represents about a quarter of the weekly national average for confectionery consumed in the 1980s. The precise ration went up and down during the course of the war, depending on supply, peaking at four ounces per week. American soldiers were issued with a daily ration of three bars of 'D-ration' chocolate. Chocolate had now been absorbed into the lives and the culture of billions of people around the world. A culture of food junkies was beginning to emerge.

# CHAPTER FOUR

# HOW CHOCOLATE IS MADE

*O tree, upraised in far off Mexicos,*
*The glory of their golden strands*
*As heavenly nectar from the chalice flows*
*Its Chocolate for other lands.*

From 'Ode to the Chocolate Tree'
By Alonsius Ferronius, a Jesuit (1664)

The eighteenth-century Swedish botanist Linnaeus (Carl von Linne) classified the cocoa tree as *Theobroma cacao*, which literally translates as 'cocoa, food for the Gods' (Greek *theos*, a god; *broma*, food). As a chocolate lover himself, he felt that the simple name 'cacao' did not do justice to the noble cocoa tree. The Aztecs, Mayans and Toltecs believed that the cocoa tree was indeed a gift from the Gods. Much ritual and ceremony was involved in its cultivation, from the planting of the seeds to the harvesting. The wild tree is said to have originated in the rich sub-canopy of virgin rain forests in the Amazon and Orinoco basins. As we have seen, it was first cultivated by Mayans on the Yucatan peninsula in Mexico, and traded with the Aztecs who lived in the drier non-cocoa-producing areas of Mexico.

Today cocoa grows throughout the tropical belt, which lies 10–20 degrees north and south of the equator. The bulk of the world's 'base' cocoa is produced in Brazil and the Gold Coast of Africa, but there are many smaller countries growing the rarer 'flavour' varieties. These are often the same countries which produce fine coffee: Bolivia, Peru, Ecuador, Colombia, Costa Rica, Cuba, Venezuela, Mexico, the Caribbean, Madagascar, the Seychelles, Sri Lanka, Malaysia, the East Indies, the Philippines and Papua New Guinea.

The cocoa tree needs constant rainfall and warmth, and when young needs to be shaded from the tropical sun and sheltered from the wind. For this reason it is frequently inter-cropped with plantains, coconut and banana trees, known as 'mother trees', or shade trees. Each cocoa-growing area has its own particular shade tree. In Trinidad, for instance, cocoa grows under the charmingly named eternal tree. If a cocoa tree is left to grow wild, without the shade and protection of a mother tree, it can reach a height of sixty feet. Apart from offering shade and protection from the elements, the mother tree also enables the cocoa tree's height to be contained at about twenty feet, which makes the harvest much easier. Orchards or groves of cocoa trees are known as 'cocoa walks'.

## THE COCOA BEAN

Chocolate comes from the fruit of the cocoa tree, and starts as a pod, containing lots of small fleshy white fruit in rows. The cocoa bean is essentially the seed germ of the fruit and looks rather like a lychee seed: small, brown, shiny and about the size and shape of an almond. The tree has the unusual habit of bearing its flowers and subsequently its pods directly on the main trunk as well as on the branches. The cocoa tree is also remarkable in that, at almost any time of the year, a close look will reveal thousands of small waxy white flowers. These blossoms are extravagant and up to fifty or even a hundred thousand can be produced by a mature tree in a single year.

*Theobroma Cocao*

Sadly the flowers have no discernible fragrance. At the same time pods of all sizes and colours and in varying degrees of ripeness can be observed.

There are two main varieties of bean, which roughly equate to coffee beans of similar quality. There are also comparisons to be made with grape varieties chosen for winemaking. The criollo beans are the quality beans, and represent only 10–15 per cent of the world's production. The criollo is the king of all cocoa beans, with a characteristic fruity flavour, and some acid. It is also known as a flavour bean, and is to chocolate what the chardonnay grape is to wine. The latter is the grape variety used for making Champagne and Chablis, the famous French white Burgundy, and is particularly favoured by US and Australian wine growers for its exceptional clean and fruity character. The criollo bean is the finest and most delicate cocoa bean in the world, but sadly it is now in danger of being replaced by the forastero.

Forastero beans are mainly grown in Africa and Brazil, and while of inferior quality they are much more robust and higher yielding than criollos. They are used either for blending or on their own, depending on the quality of the end product. The forastero is a rather bland but high yielding bean, producing 'base' cocoa, and is generally roasted at a very high temperature in order to disguise its inadequacies. It is used for all mass-produced chocolate, and sometimes blended with flavour beans such as criollo and trinitario.

There are also a number of hybrid beans, of which the trinitario is the best known. It is said to be the result of a natural hybridization between the criollo and forastero, which took place after a hurricane in Trinidad in 1727. It inherits the genetic resistance of the forastero plant, and the delicate flavour of the criollo. The trinitario is a mellow bean, with a variety of characteristics, which range from newly-mown hay, oak and honey, to balsamic. It is mainly used for blending.

## THE COCOA HARVEST

The cocoa tree starts to bear fruit in its fourth or fifth year, and can continue to produce crops for thirty years. The harvest comes twice a year, as soon as the pods become ripe and golden. The main harvest takes place before the dry season, the second, smaller one at the end of the rainy season. The pods are cut straight from the tree trunks with machetes, great care being taken not to damage the bark of the tree. This process is extremely labour intensive and requires great skill, so the cocoa harvest provides much seasonal work. The price of labour in the cocoa-growing areas might be considered low by western standards, but with so many workers needed, the harvest represents a large proportion of chocolate production costs.

Each tree produces between fifty and one hundred cocoa pods a year, but by the time the beans are shipped, the dried yield from one tree will weigh approximately three pounds. The harvested cocoa pods are sliced open to reveal a cluster of fleshy white fruit, not dissimilar to a mangosteen or lychee. The fruit is placed in vats, and the white flesh – which is naturally high in sugar – precipitates fermentation, a critical stage in the development of the characteristic aroma, flavour and colour of chocolate. The outer pods are often used as fibrous animal feed.

At the end of the fermentation process, the sweet white flesh has been transformed into acetic acid, and has evaporated. The beans are now light brown in colour, and are known as green cocoa beans. The next stage is drying, and ideally they should be allowed to dry naturally in the open air, but this can present a problem because rainfall in the cocoa belt is very high. Specially constructed roofs on rollers are used (rather like the ones used to cover the wicket on cricket pitches), which are pulled over to cover the beans when the rain comes. In Trinidad the women perform a cocoa dance, which involves shuffling across the beans to ensure that they are evenly turned. The thoroughly dried beans (now weighing only about a quarter of their harvested weight) are sorted to remove any

bad beans and packed into 50kg sacks, ready to be shipped to the chocolate factory, which is most likely to be in Europe or America. Among the world's biggest factories are Hershey in the United States, Cadbury in the United Kingdom, Côte d'Or and Callebaut in Belgium, Nestlé and Lindt in Switzerland, and Droste in Holland.

It seems that the cooler the climate, the higher the consumption of the finished product. In the league table of chocolate consumption among the Europeans, the Swiss take the lead with an annual average of 9.8kg (21.5lbs) per head per annum. They are followed by the Norwegians, who consume 8kg (17.6lbs). In joint third place are the British and Belgians, with 7.4kg (16.25lbs), followed by Germany, Holland, Ireland and Denmark. The French, surprisingly, seem to eat fairly small quantities, a meagre 4kg (8.8lbs). Italy, Greece, Spain and Portugal consume less than 2kg (4.4lbs) per head per annum – despite Spain's crucial early role in promulgating chocolate!

When the beans arrive at their final destination, they undergo further sorting and checking. In the factory the beans are carefully roasted, to achieve a fine delicate aroma. If cocoa beans are roasted for too long, a smoky flavour pervades the finished chocolate. Manufacturers who wish to keep the cocoa content of their chocolate low, yet achieve a strong and bitter flavour, tend to give the beans a long roasting.

The next process is known as winnowing; in which the outer skin of the cocoa bean is blown away, to leave the cocoa nib. Some manufacturers keep the husks from the winnowed beans, and press 'shell butter' from them (a very soft, low-quality cocoa butter), while others pack them up as mulch for gardeners. The latter use is preferable in my opinion, as not only are the by-products recycled, but a delicious aroma of cocoa wafts up from the flower beds!

The nibs are then ground, by passing them through a series of rollers, to a particle size of 50–70 microns. At this stage they are large enough to be discernibly coarse and gritty. The heat which results from the pressure of the rollers causes the cocoa butter to melt and so the cocoa bean divides into its two constituent parts: cocoa mass (or liquor) and cocoa butter. This system was first developed by Van Houten in the early nineteenth century. Before Van Houten's invention, excess cocoa butter floating to the surface of hot chocolate drinks was a constant problem, often remedied by the addition of cornmeal, flour or other absorbent products. There were some cases of large-scale adulteration of cocoa, and there is even evidence of brick dust and more poisonous substances such as red lead having been used.

# 'GRAND CRU' CHOCOLATES

At the nibbing stage, the different beans are blended to create cuveés. A cuveé is the term used to describe what happens when wine makers blend two or more grape varieties, which have been chosen for their complementary character-istics. The process is used particularly when blending a champagne and is similar to the art of the parfumier in creating a perfume. A notable specialist chocolate producer is Valrhona, based in the Rhone Valley, in France. There they take a special pride in the art of fine chocolate making. Their attention to detail is uncompromising, and they have a panel of twelve chocolate experts who meet every day and taste the different 'Grand Cru' chocolates to ensure their consistency and quality.

Unlike wines, which vary according to the year in which they were harvested, cocoa beans do not normally suffer from weather fluctuations. The period of time which elapses between the harvesting of the raw cocoa and the manufacture of a bar of chocolate is usually a matter of weeks rather than months, but dried cocoa beans can be stored for a long time in a controlled environment; and careful blending ensures that each vat of the world's finest chocolate has a predictable flavour, texture and aroma.

After the cocoa butter has been pressed from the cocoa mass, there is a parting of the ways: the industrial manufacturers separate the two parts, for cocoa butter commands a high price on the open market, being much sought after by the pharmaceutical and cosmetics industries. It is a unique fat because it is solid at 33°C (91.4°F), but melts at 34°C (93.2°F) just below blood temperature 37°C (98.6°F), which makes it ideal as a base for lipstick, among other things. This century has seen the invention of a number of cocoa butter substitutes, or 'enhancers' as they are also called in the trade. They are used to replace cocoa butter in the manufacturing of chocolate. Personally, whatever reasons the industrial manufacturers give to justify the process on commercial grounds, I do not believe that there is a satisfactory substitute for pure unadulterated cocoa butter. Nevertheless, it is common practice to sell off at least part of the cocoa butter and replace it with different sorts of 'butter' fat, derived from various nut and palm oils.

The other important difference between mass-produced chocolate and artisan chocolate is the addition of artificial vanilla, known as vanillin. Some would say that it is indistinguishable from the real McCoy, and perhaps if it were used with a little subtlety, it might be hard to tell the difference, but in my experience it is usually obvious just from the aroma of the chocolate. The tradition of adding vanilla to chocolate goes back to Cortés, and many chocolate makers believe that our palates are now so accustomed to that flavour that chocolate would taste very strange without it. The smaller specialist producers, on the other hand, still prefer to mix the cocoa mass and cocoa butter back together, adding a little

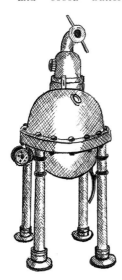

sugar, powdered or condensed milk (if it is to be milk chocolate), and pure vanilla. It was Henri Nestlé and Daniel Peter, at Vevey in Switzerland, who perfected the technique of using evaporated milk, so that it could be incorporated into solid chocolate. The mixture is then further ground to a particle size of 18–20 microns, which is indiscernible to the palate.

The next stage is where the conching takes place. The conching machine was invented in 1880 by another Swiss pioneer, Rodolfe Lindt. The name derives from the shape of his prototype, which was a large, shell-shaped vessel. It works by grinding the chocolate between granite rollers to create a very smooth, velvety texture. The effect of conching is to refine the chocolate and remove any residual bitterness. Before the invention of conching, eating chocolate would have been very rough and gritty in the mouth, and would not have had the sensual qualities of present-day fine chocolate.

Conching is a process which ought not be hurried, yet for the cheaper chocolate bars this stage is often cut down to the minimum time, that is about twelve hours. Other producers allow conching to continue for up to seven days, adding extra cocoa butter in order to make the finished chocolate even smoother, and to give it greater fluidity. This is an important factor when it is to be used for dipping chocolate, making bonbons, truffles, mousses and so on. The name of this quality of chocolate is 'couverture', from the French word meaning covering. In translation the word brings to mind all the worst sorts of chocolate cake coverings which in some cases contain no real chocolate at all; just fats, sugar and flavouring. By contrast the French term 'couverture' is a very precise one: it means a chocolate with at least 32 per cent cocoa butter. Any chocolate bar meeting this specification will not only be good to cook with, but will also make excellent eating.

## READING CHOCOLATE LABELS

An area of confusion when reading chocolate labels is the use of the words cocoa liquor and cocoa solids. The Americans favour the word cocoa liquor, and the Europeans cocoa solids. They both mean the entire cocoa content, including the cocoa butter. Cocoa nibs (cocoa beans with the husk removed) comprise 53 per cent fat in the form of cocoa butter, and 47 per cent dry matter, or cocoa mass. When the nibs are ground down, cocoa liquor is made. Cocoa content (cocoa liquor or solids) is normally expressed as a percentage of the net weight. Today we have bars ranging from 15 per cent cocoa solids, which in my mind do not deserve to be called chocolate, to unsweetened chocolate weighing in at 99 per cent cocoa solids, which I find equally unpalatable. The French chocolatier Michel Chaudun, (himself described as being to chocolate what Descartes is to philosophy), says that sugar is to chocolate what salt is to other foods. In other words, a little will enhance, too much will destroy the flavour.

The Americans are far more exacting about labelling regulations than the Europeans, who seem unable to agree on definitions. In the early days of the European Common Market, several member states, notably the French and Germans, called for British chocolate to be renamed 'vegolate', because of its low cocoa content and the addition of vegetable fats other than cocoa butter. The American Food and Drug Administration is very precise in its definitions and labelling requirements. Wherever optional ingredients for flavouring are used, they must be declared conspicuously. These include: spice, pure vanilla, vanillin and other artificial flavours, butter, milk fat, coffee, nuts and salt. So in America one can see labels like this: 'Chocolate with added cinnamon, vanilla and ethyl vanillin, an artificial flavoring.' When cocoa powder has undergone the 'Dutching' process, it also has to state 'Processed with alkali' or detail which specific alkali has been used. There are also very precise categories for different types of chocolate: the FDA regulations state that 'sweet' chocolate must contain not less than 15 per cent cocoa liquor (cocoa solids), that 'bittersweet' chocolate must contain not less than 35 per cent cocoa liquor. Milk chocolate must contain not less than 3.66 per cent milk fat, not less than 12 per cent milk solids, and should be not less than 10 per cent of the weight of the cocoa liquor. There are also reams about the addition of dextrose, corn syrup and dried glucose, which all have specified maximum levels. Thus American consumers are given far more information about exactly what goes into their chocolate bars than anyone else in the world.

To distinguish between low-grade commercial chocolate and premium chocolate, an informed customer can discover most of the important factors from the ingredients list on the back of the wrapper. The first point to look for is the cocoa content, which means the combined total of cocoa butter and cocoa solids. This should be at least 50 per cent if it is plain chocolate, or 30 per cent if it is milk chocolate. If sugar is high on the contents list, warning bells should be set off, because it constitutes the balance of the ingredients. The quality and variety of the cocoa beans and the level of roasting are not things that one can easily discover from the labelling, except in France, where the use of the term 'fine cocoa' is strictly controlled, and refers only to the rarer cocoa beans such as criollo and trinitario. The cocoa butter content is sometimes listed separately, especially on couverture.

The use of cocoa butter substitutes (CBSs) is harder to spot immediately, but any mention of vegetable or animal fats would indicate their use. Any residual greasiness in the mouth comes from CBSs, which are among the very few vegetable fats which are saturated, and have the same undesirable effects on blood cholesterol levels as animal fats. In the UK it is permissible to add up to 5 per cent CBSs without mentioning them on the list of ingredients.

Another ingredient used almost universally is lecithin, an emulsifier derived from the soya bean which counteracts moisture and helps to stabilize chocolate. It is a product sold in health food shops, naturally high in vitamin E, and there is nothing particularly sinister about it.

The next question is whether pure vanilla has been used, or artificial vanilla (vanillin). When the word 'flavouring' is used, it can be safely assumed that the vanilla is artificial, as anyone using pure vanilla is certain to state the fact. Pure vanilla, often listed as 'Vanille Bourbon', comes from an orchid grown in Madagascar. Other undesirable features to be aware of when tasting chocolate are burnt smoky flavours and overwhelming sweetness.

VANILLE

## HOW TO TASTE CHOCOLATE

To become an expert in chocolate tasting, all that is required is a love of chocolate, a palate which has not been dulled by too much sugar, and the ability to compare and contrast. There is an obvious comparison with wine. Most of us have graduated from the unsophisticated phase, where sugar and fizz are all-important, to the point where we are able to appreciate good wine, even if we find it hard to describe. At wine tastings, each glass of wine is examined for colour and density and turned in circular movements, to allow the bouquet to rise up and stimulate the olfactory senses, before the liquid is run over the taste buds. With chocolate it is a little different, because we are dealing with a solid material. However, as with wine, there is more to chocolate tasting than just taste. Indeed, with chocolate all five senses come into play:

**Touch** The point to observe is the speed of melting (the quicker the better – this indicates a high cocoa butter content). Chocolate should start to melt if held in the hand for a few seconds, because of the unique qualities of cocoa butter as a fat mentioned earlier. It is solid up to 33°C (91.4°F) and molten at 34°C (93.2°F).

**Sound** It is the crystalline structure of cocoa butter which gives real chocolate its distinctive crisp snap, with a texture of tree bark in the break.

**Sight** Gloss and condition can be quickly assessed just by looking at a piece of chocolate. When a 'bloom' is observed it is generally caused either by heat or by moisture. The first type is normally referred to as a 'cocoa butter bloom', and indicates that the chocolate was not tempered correctly or that it has been allowed to get too warm and then cool down again. The cocoa butter crystals rise to the surface and re-crystallize. This does not always affect the flavour of the chocolate, but should be seen as a warning that it was not stored in ideal conditions. It can be rectified by tempering the chocolate again, thus realigning the crystalline structure. The second kind of bloom is referred to as a 'sugar bloom'. If moisture is allowed to settle on the surface of chocolate, which can happen when it is stored in a damp atmosphere, it draws the sugar crystals up to the surface. The sugar then dissolves in the water, and later re-crystallizes on the surface, destroying the texture of the chocolate. The whole appearance and texture will be grey and gritty, and the only place for it is in the dustbin! So be careful when storing chocolate in the fridge; it is best kept in an air-tight container. With regard to colour in general, the redder and lighter the cocoa, the finer the flavour.

**Smell** Without a sense of smell, all is lost. It is the nose which is the most highly tuned instrument for the delectation of any food or wine. As with tasting, too much sugar interferes with the process, just as too much salt can overwhelm delicate flavours. Smoking dulls the palate, as do very strong flavours such as peppermint and chilli, and this affects our sense of smell as well as our ability to taste.

**Taste** Although we do not spit out the chocolate, as the wine buffs do, neither do we *eat* it. A small piece of the chocolate should be placed on the tongue and allowed to melt of its own accord. I suggest that three or four bars are tried side by side, with a glass of water to sip between samples.

Professional chocolate tasters often use a vocabulary that is borrowed from wine tasters. 'Notes', or characteristics, are looked for, and expressed in comparisons with, for example, flower blossoms, citrus and red berry fruits, newly mown hay and green tea. With a little practice we all develop a method of tasting that works for us, and learn to recognize the different characteristics of the chocolates we taste. One thing that all fine chocolate has in common, like great wines, is a very long 'finish'.

We need to learn to be discriminating about chocolate quality. In the last hundred years the chocolate industry has been revolutionized, and as with all revolutions, much care needs to be taken to ensure that corruption does not set in. The more expertise we have, the more influence we can wield. As consumers we have the right to demand higher standards from the manufacturers, and they would be foolish not to take note.

There is now a growing trend in the food industry as a whole to increase product awareness, and improve the quality of merchandise. The public is demanding more information about exact ingredients and additives, and is moving towards a better position from which to make an informed choice. There is still a tendency to sacrifice quality for price. In the final analysis, each person must decide whether to consume mass-produced chocolate, laden with additives and sugar, or to demand the finer and rarer cocoa bean varieties from which the finest chocolate is made.

CHAPTER FIVE

# A LITTLE OF WHAT
# YOU FANCY

**T**o some a poison, to others an elixir, chocolate was an
important source of nourishment for the ancient tribes
of America, including the great Aztec civilization, in which it
was highly valued for its sustaining properties. The Aztecs
would march all day on a single cup of *xocolatl*.

In his book *Native Races of the Pacific States*, published in
1875, the historian H. H. Bancroft wrote about the Aztecs,
and other Native American peoples who used chocolate as a
medicine. There is a fascinating account of how the Aztecs,
'. . . dug up the bones of giants at the foot of the mountains,
and collected by their dwarfish successors, ground to powder,
mixed with Cocoa, and drunk as a cure for diarrhoea and
dysentery.' This seems to echo the Chinese tradition of digging
up 'dragon' bones, to be ground and mixed with other herbs as
a medicine, adding weight to the theory that the early settlers
of America originally came from Asia. A bit later Bancroft
writes: 'Scalding hot Cocoa mixed with chilli is the favourite
stimulant, of which very large quantities are imbibed, until the
perspiration starts from every pore.'

In 1604 Joseph Acosta wrote of chocolate as being good for
the stomach and for catarrh. Thirty years later Thomas Gage,

the mendicant friar, paid his native porters in chocolate. This served as a wonderfully refreshing and energizing drink, which the Indians regarded very highly, as well as having another value in the form of money, so that everyone was well pleased with the exchange. Gage attributed his own excellent health to having drunk five cups of chocolate every day for twelve years. He also found it gave him the energy to stay awake at night to write his notes.

As early as 1631, Antonio Colmenero published the first recipe for drinking chocolate. He had himself taken the recipe from a physician in Marchena:

> *Of cacaos 700 (beans)*
> *Of white sugar, one pound and a halfe*
> *Cinnamon 2 ounces*
> *Of long red pepper 14*
> *Of cloves, halfe an ounce (the best writers use them not)*
> *Three Cods of the Logwood or Campeche tree. These*
> *    Cods are very good, and smell like Fennell.*
> *or instead of that the Weight of 2 Reals or a shilling of*
> *    Anniseeds.*
> *As much of Achiote as will give it colour which is*
> *    about the quantity of a hasell-nut.*

Colmenero later comments that to his mind this quantity of achiote is too little to colour the quantity made according to the Marchena recipe, and he suggests each person should put in as much as he thinks fit, a suggestion which future cookery writers would express in the formula 'according to taste'. Achiote is still used today, especially in the Caribbean and the Philippines. More commonly known as *anatto*, it is a kind of seed, and serves as a natural, red colouring agent.

He goes on to discuss the virtues of this drink, which is so wholesome and so good. He explains that there are two sorts of cocoa: one is common, and is made from cocoa beans which are a grey colour, inclining towards red; the other is made from a broader and bigger bean, known as '*patlaxte*'. This bean is white and more drying, and also it causes insomnia, and therefore is not as useful as the first variety. The two different

bean varieties to which he was referring may well have been *criollo* and *forastero*. It is indeed true that cocoa stimulates the brain, owing to the theobromine naturally present in the bean, and therefore might cause insomnia. The idea of taking hot chocolate as a bedtime drink seems to be a twentieth-century one, and works because, while the cocoa may serve as a stimulant, the hot milk acts as a calming sleep inducer.

He also mentions some of the ingredients which were commonly added to the drink. He writes approvingly of the effect of adding almonds, and with great disapproval of the adulteration of the drink with maize. This was a habit of the natives, possibly because they liked the mixture or else, as Colmenero believed, an economy made for the sake of profit. The following passage contains what must be one of the earliest references to the evils of adulteration:

> Some put in Almonds, kernels of Nuts, and Orange-flower water. They do not ill because they give it more body and substance than maize or

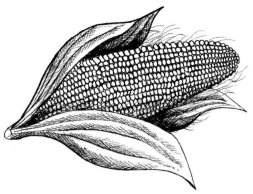

*Paniso, which others use, and for my part I should always put it into Chocolate, for almonds are moderately hot and have a thin juice; but you must not use new almonds. . . . Those who mix maize, or Paniso in the Chocolate do very ill; because those grains do beget a very melancholy Humour. It is also apparently windy, and those which mix it in this confection, do it only for their profit, by increasing the quantity of the chocolate.*

He also detailed at some length the various types of chillies which were commonly added to the drink. Mexico is still famous for its many chilli varieties, the best known being the jalapeño, which becomes the chipotle when smoke dried; then come the ancho, pasilla and serrano. In Colmenero's day there were four types of red peppers used in flavouring chocolate.

*Two kinds are very quick and biting, the other two are called Tonalchiles, and these are moderately hot; for, they are eaten with bread, as they eat other fruits, and they are of a yellow colour; and they grow only about the Towns, which they are in, and adjoining to the Lake of Mexico. The other pepper is called Chilpaclagua, which hath a broad husk and is not so biting as the first, nor so gentle as the last, and is that which is usually put in chocolate. There are also other ingredients . . . one called Mechasuchil, another Vinecaxtli, which in Spanish they call Orejuelas, which are sweet smelling flowers, Aromacticall and hot. In Spain they put in powder of Roses of*

*Alexandria. I have spoken of all these ingredients,
that everyone may make choice of those that please
him best, or are most proper for his infirmities. The
cacao is mingled with all these ingredients which are
hot, which serve to temper the coldnesse of the cacao.*

When speaking of coldness, Colmenero is referring to one of
the key classifications used in medieval medicine. The
concepts of hot and cold did not relate to the actual
temperature at which the food would have been eaten, but
rather to its 'energetic' nature. For example, melon would be
seen as being cold, and ginger as hot. These classifications
were closely associated with the idea of the body being
composed of humours (which are essentially 'energies'
transported by the blood and body fluids) which, if not kept in
balance, cause illness. The medieval apothecary's job was to
prescribe herbs of different 'energies' to correct an excess or
lack of any humour and thus bring his patient back to health.
This age-old principle is still being followed today in some
branches of 'alternative' medicine, notably traditional Chinese
herbal medicine and acupuncture, which have a 2,000-year
history of practice and theoretical debate, and pre-date the
discovery of chocolate by some fifteen centuries.

It is not surprising, with such an attitude prevailing, that
Spanish physicians condemned the practice of taking cold
chocolate, since it was already considered 'cold' in the
energetic sense. In the seventeenth century a new craze for
'The Gallants and the Ladies' was for drinks to be refrigerated
in snow, especially chocolate. Perhaps this should be seen as a
precursor of the modern chocolate milk shake?

One of the earliest known users of cocoa in France was
Cardinal Richelieu's brother, Alphonse-Louis du Plessis. He
took cocoa as a medicine, after consulting his physician René
Moreau about its therapeutic qualities. In 1661 the French
faculty of medicine approved the use of chocolate. At this time
cocoa was still unknown in the French provinces. In 1672
Madame de Sévigné was devastated to learn that her daughter

was going to live in Lyons, a city which had no chocolate maker. Today Lyons is the second city of France, a great gastronomic centre, and boasts hundreds of artisan *chocolatiers*. One is the renowned Monsieur Bernachon, who actually manufactures small quantities of chocolate, from raw cocoa beans, in his *atelier*.

For a short time in the mid-seventeenth century, chocolate went out of fashion at the French court, having been blamed for causing 'vapours' and palpitations. But at the same time in the English court of Charles II it was highly regarded. The court physician Henry Stubbe wrote *The Indian Nectar* in praise of chocolate. His opinion on the health value of chocolate was that it was nourishing, but too much sugar or spice was not good. He himself made the finest chocolate for the King's use.

As we have seen, the diarist Samuel Pepys, having drunk too much on the day of the coronation ceremonies, took chocolate on 24 April 1661, 'to settle my stomach'. His doctor, Sir Hans Sloane (1660–1753), who was also physician to Queen Anne and George II, thought highly of chocolate's restorative qualities. Born in Ireland, Sir Hans was evidently a great physician and intellectual, studying in Paris and Montpelier, and travelling to Jamaica, where he collected over 800 specimens of plants. It was there that he first recognized the therapeutic qualities of chocolate. He saw malnourished, sickly babies revive after taking a mixture of cocoa, and he is generally credited with being the first person to try mixing it with milk. However it seems that Sloane's chocolate recipe was being marketed purely as a medicine. The recipe for the remedy was a closely guarded secret, which Sloane sold to an apothecary called Nicholas Sanders. Sanders had a shop at No. 8 Greek Street, in London's Soho. The business, together with the secret recipe, were then sold to one William White. Through this connection, the Cadbury brothers eventually came to own the recipe, and they used it in their early pioneering of the highly profitable drinking chocolate market from the 1820s onwards.

By 1685 cocoa was already accepted by most physicians as being nutritious. It was widely used by the gentry, medicinally as well as socially. By the early-eighteenth century, quacks were beginning to take advantage of this reputation. In the *Tatler* newspaper (Issue No. 97) in 1709, a certain Mr Lawrence advertised: 'Chemical quintessence of Bohee-Tea, and Cocoa-Nuts where in the volatile salts, oil and spirit of them both are chemically extracted and united.' This medicine was to be obtained at his toyshop, at the sign of the Griffin in the Poultry, London.

Some physicians held strong opinions about the use of chocolate as a medicine. Dr Duncan, of the faculty of Montpelier, in France, noted in 1706 that coffee, chocolate and tea served a purpose as medicines '. . . while [unsweetened] they continued unpleasant, but once they were made delicious with sugar, they are become poison.' If a few more people had shared the far-sighted Dr Duncan's opinion, we might not have been left the legacy of over-sugared chocolate bars today. The main reason for this practice was an economic one. Sugar is considerably cheaper than cocoa, especially if produced from sugar beet, rather than sugar cane.

The reputed 'medicinal' effect of chocolate also found its way into folklore and superstition. Chocolate was supposed to be good for pregnant women, and in the eighteenth century one man described how after drinking chocolate his wife had three times given birth to twins. Madame de Sévigné indulged in a bit of scandal regarding chocolate in one of her letters. She reported that the Marquise de Coetlogon had given birth to a baby, reputed to be 'black as an Indian', apparently after drinking too much chocolate. Possibly the writer had her tongue in her cheek, knowing that another explanation was more probable.

By the nineteenth century, the image had changed slightly, and cocoa was now considered to be very much a man's drink, appreciated by hunters and soldiers. Conan Doyle chose it for Sherlock Holmes's breakfast. Cocoa certainly seems to have stood 'real men' in good stead, fortifying the mind, body and spirit.

Chocolate, too, has been greatly appreciated by men who have had to perform arduous tasks in the most extreme conditions of cold intensified by wind – none more so than arctic explorers and mountain climbers. Chocolate is the ideal emergency ration, because it offers instant energy, conveniently packaged. The 1924 Everest expedition carried plain chocolate, as well as supplies of nutmilk, vanilla, coffee and so on. When Sir Edmund Hillary conquered Everest in 1953, he was sustained by chocolate. One wonders whether Sherpa Tensing also developed a taste for it. . . .

Cocoa has been drunk by British sailors for over 200 years. The tradition began in 1780, when British ships were stationed in Antigua, at the centre of the cocoa-producing West Indies. A Royal Navy captain, James Ferguson, enjoyed the chocolate himself, and realized that this nutritious drink would be a valuable addition to the diet of men stationed in the West Indies. As it was locally produced, it had the additional advantage of being a cheap form of nutrition.

Later, Surgeon Trotter recommended that cocoa should also be given to the men in the Channel fleet. The coldness of these northern seas would have made cocoa even more welcome. In 1823 a ration of one ounce of cocoa per man per day was extended to the whole navy. The navy rum ration has been much publicized, but the less spectacular cocoa ration should take credit for building up the strength of ordinary seamen. Those who went to sea in the eighteenth century were often puny men who could find no other means of livelihood, many being press-ganged into service.

Until quite recently the Royal Navy used chocolate only in the old block form, which was full of cocoa butter and required grating into cups. The navy remained untouched by the nineteenth-century technology which produces today's refined cocoa powder. Only in 1968 was the fatty chocolate block withdrawn and replaced by refined cocoa powder, no doubt to the dismay of some old-timers who appreciated the cocoa butter fat that warmed them on cold wet watches.

It is an astonishing fact that over half of the cocoa imported into England in the nineteenth century was consumed by the Royal Navy! The tradition continues in the military to this day, especially among the Americans who make sure that a Hershey bar is included in all army campaign rations. Recently the space scientists based at NASA have invested considerable sums of money in chocolate technology. They share the opinion that chocolate is the perfect, highly concentrated, nutritious, yet delicious food.

Chocolate has been an important part of our heritage for over a hundred years, and has now become inextricably linked with

many of the ancient pagan and Christian feasts and fasts. Imagine Easter without chocolate eggs and bunnies! The rites of spring had been celebrated for thousands of years before the crucifixion of Jesus. In Roman times, Eostre, the goddess of dawn, represented spring and new life. Arriving each year on the vernal equinox, she was reputed to have taken the form of a hare, in order to distribute eggs around the countryside. Our modern day Easter egg hunts clearly have a distinguished ancestry.

In some countries chocolate is associated with other feasts and holidays. In Japan as in the United States, one of the most popular times for giving chocolate is St Valentine's Day. The

Japanese have adapted this western tradition. On 14 February girls give chocolate hearts to their loved one, and the gesture is reciprocated by the menfolk one month later on 'Howaito' (White) Day. There is also a custom called 'giri choco' (literally 'duty chocolate'), which entails employees giving chocolates to their managers as a token of loyalty. In Holland the feast of St Nicholas, or Santa Claus, is celebrated on 6 December. All the children put out clogs to be filled by Santa with chocolate money, providing that they have been good. The idea of eating or being given chocolate as a reward has become firmly embedded in our culture.

Since cocoa became a part of European life, there have even been various conflicting papal rulings about chocolate. The first pope who tasted the drink found it so disgusting that he felt it unnecessary to ban it. Others felt that, as a drink, it did not contravene the rigorous Lenten fasting laws. Others again deemed it to be a food. There is no doubt that part of the appeal of chocolate for many people is that it is forbidden and in some sense naughty.

Since Van Houten and Lindt's contributions to chocolate technology, the introduction of chocolate moulds has been universal. Some of the most charming ones were made at the end of the nineteenth century, when the business of moulding chocolate was on a very small scale. Typically a specialist baker and confectioner would make a small amount of chocolate each day, and as all the moulds were filled by hand, it was possible to use lots of different forms. The French mould catalogue which appears on the endpapers in this book is full of weird and wonderful shapes, all of which were available off the shelf. Nowadays, as things scale up, we are left with much less choice; market forces determine which are the best-selling lines. There also seems to be a propensity towards rather kitsch cartoon character models, in place of the more realistic hares and other creatures from bygone years.

Cocoa seems to have been used widely from the middle of the nineteenth century onwards, and appears in the nutritional expert, Sir Jack Drummond's, list of the food items in a typical poor man's diet in 1939. They were: 2oz of sausages, 4oz of potatoes, 24oz of white bread, 1oz of margarine, 2oz of jam, 1oz of cocoa, 1oz of condensed milk with tea, and 2oz of sugar. The equivalent list that he gives for the middle class also contains 1oz of cocoa, which shows that by 1939 the food value of cocoa was recognized by most British people. The custom at this time was to eat a high tea, and to drink a cup of cocoa before going to bed to ensure a good night's sleep. In World War II, as we have seen, the nutritional value of chocolate was recognized by its inclusion in the rationing schemes of several of the countries allied against the Germans.

The effects of chocolate on health have been debated for centuries. It has been accused at various times of causing migraines, pimples, obesity, tooth decay and even *crises de foie* (liver attacks – which seem to be a uniquely French ailment). These claims, I am glad to say, can now be seen as the myths they are. Hervé Robert, a French doctor, has done extensive research on the subject, and in his recent book *Les Vertus Thérapeutiques du Chocolat* has published the results of his own and other surveys into the effects of chocolate eating.

Robert concedes that there is a tenuous link between chocolate and migraine: 'Chocolate contains a small quantity of tyramine, which in large doses can cause migraine. However, it is also present in far larger amounts in Roquefort, Camembert and other fermented cheeses. If chocolate is eaten after a heavy meal where red wine and cheese have also been consumed, the tiny amount of tyramine present in the chocolate may act as the trigger for a migraine, but only as the last straw that broke the camel's back. So it would be true to say that chocolate by itself does not cause migraine.'

On the subject of acne, he refers to extensive surveys carried out in the United States which have concluded that there is no connection between chocolate consumption and spots in teenagers. He also maintains that those who blame chocolate for acne or migraines take no account of hormone imbalances, which may well be responsible for both ills. Often, for example, the sort of young person who suffers from skin problems does not have the healthiest lifestyle. Other factors such as lack of sleep, too much greasy food, not enough fresh fruit and vegetables, and too many junk chocolate bars – eaten as an instant energy fix in place of proper meals – are all likely to result in oily skin and spots.

The causes of migraine are often very similar. When a busy individual is working under stress, it may only be after many hours of frenzied mental activity that the realization comes of having missed a meal – or even several. Often one of the first things that come to hand is a very sugary bar of 'junk' chocolate. Any of these, either separately or together, may act as the final trigger, but certainly none of them would cause a problem when eaten as part of a sensible diet.

When I refer to 'junk chocolate', I mean the mass-produced, mass-marketed bars that contain very little cocoa, sometimes so little that it is not even included as a percentage in the list of ingredients. Really good plain chocolate should contain at least 50 per cent cocoa solids. In milk chocolate the cocoa solids ought to represent at least 30 per cent of the ingredients.

Fine chocolate, with cocoa solids above 50 per cent, can be a valuable part of a balanced diet, as it is naturally high in nutriments; it contains cocoa butter (which helps to lower the blood cholesterol levels), calcium, potassium, sodium, magnesium, iron, theobromine (a stimulant similar to caffeine), and vitamins A1, B1, B2, C, D and E. Robert also states that diabetics may safely eat small amounts of chocolate, so long as it contains a minimum of 60 per cent cocoa solids.

Phenylethylamine, which is the naturally occurring ingredient in chocolate most often blamed for causing addiction, acts in a similar way to an amphetamine; it is an anti-depressant, which stimulates the brain and creates a state of euphoria similar to that of being in love. Perhaps this accounts for the familiar image of the love-lorn woman languishing in her boudoir, consuming boxes of chocolate creams. Casanova is said to have rated chocolate above champagne for its seductive and aphrodisiac qualities.

The chemical composition of theobromine in cocoa is almost identical to that of caffeine in coffee and theine in tea, and has similar effects. Like them it is an alkaloid which stimulates brain and muscle performance and gives a boost to counteract fatigue. In small doses it is certainly not harmful. The amount of this stimulant ingested through eating a moderate amount of chocolate would equate to the caffeine absorbed when drinking a moderate amount of coffee.

Sugar, of course, is held responsible for a number of our western ailments. On the subject of tooth decay and chocolate, however, Robert is once again reassuring:

'While it is accepted that the sugar content in chocolate encourages dental caries, the cocoa itself contains at least three substances which kill the streptococcal bacteria that lead to the formation of dental plaque.'

He also points out that when dentists classify foods which are most likely to lead to tooth decay, they place grapes, bananas, chips, cereal bars and bread above sugar. Chocolate comes below all of these!

The amount of sugar we absorb from chocolate depends entirely on the kind and amount of chocolate we eat. Chocolate with a high cocoa content, and therefore low in sugar, will not cause the great surges in the blood sugar levels which are probably the main reason for chocolate bingeing and addiction. Similarly, most of the additives found in junk chocolate are notably absent in really good-quality chocolate. In general it would be true to say that, with chocolate as with so much else, you get what you pay for. Don't be put off buying very expensive bars, because with the best chocolate you will find that you need to eat much less of it.

So the moral of the story is that one should be discriminating about chocolate, learn to appreciate the best, and when buying it go for quality, not quantity. Good chocolate, eaten in sensible amounts, is not fattening, does not cause spots or migraines, and is a uniquely satisfying and sensual food. In fact it will do you good, so enjoy it!

RECIPES

**O**nly the very finest chocolate should be used for cooking. It is even more true when cooking with chocolate than it is with wine, for example, that the finer the ingredients, the better the end result.

I recommend Valrhona as the greatest chocolate producer in the world. Its chocolate is chosen by many of the world's leading pastry chefs and is available through most good specialist stores, or by mail order from the Chocolate Society in England (page 119). Failing that, I would use Lindt Excellence of Surfin, Charbonnel et Walker's Chocolat Fondant or Cote d'Or Extra Amer. Nestlé also do a good *chocolat patissier*, and Callebaut's couverture is very good where it is available, which is normally only to professional chefs.

In general, the word "couverture" is a good indication of high quality, but do not be confused by words such as "covering" or "coating" chocolate, which refer to a completely different and inferior product. Look for chocolate containing a high proportion of cocoa solids, and pure vanilla extract (essence), not vanillin, an artificial flavouring.

**Melting:** When melting chocolate, it is best to use a bain-marie, or a double boiler. This is a French invention, and it is simply a pan of hot or simmering water with a bowl suspended over it. It is used for making delicate sauces, custards and for melting chocolate, which direct heat would damage or burn. Only use a bain-marie if the bowl makes a proper seal with the pan of water underneath. If a small bowl is left to stand in the middle of a large pan of simmering water, steam may contaminate the chocolate, and even a small amount of water or steam ruins good chocolate. If you do not have a proper bain-marie, a useful addition to any kitchen is a large stainless steel bowl, available from any good cookware shop or catering supply store, which works just as well. Placed over a pan of hot water, it is cheaper and more versatile than a bain-marie. Just make sure the bowl overlaps the sides of the pan, creating a good seal. In fact, all the chocolate chefs I have seen doing demonstrations favour this method.

When using a bain-marie or stainless steel bowl for melting chocolate, the water in the pan should not boil, and rarely needs to exceed 140°F (60°C). This is because most chocolate becomes molten at 113-131°F (45–55°C). Chocolate burns very easily and at surprisingly low temperatures. Milk and white chocolates are particularly susceptible, because they contain the milk protein casein, which denatures at 129°F (54°C) – even lower than the temperature at which some bittersweet (dark) chocolate melts.

It is possible to use a microwave to melt chocolate, but be very careful. Choose the lowest possible setting, and after an initial period of 30 seconds, use short bursts of 10 seconds, checking after each burst to see whether the chocolate has melted.

For those of you with a plate-warming oven, chocolate can be left to melt very slowly and gently overnight. However, you need to know your oven well to have the confidence to do this. Alternatively, chop the chocolate into squares and put into an ovenproof dish. Place the dish low down in the oven, set at the lowest temperature, and leave for about 15 minutes. The chocolate will retain its shape even when melted, so test it with a fork. I find this last method to be the simplest and best.

Other utensils which are useful for working with chocolate include a good balloon whisk and a couple of plastic spatulas.

**Tempering:** Tempered chocolate is used for coating truffles and for moulding chocolate. Without becoming too technical, it is possible to temper chocolate at home with a standard candy (sugar) thermometer.

Melt about two-thirds of the chocolate in a bain-marie until fluid, 118–131°F (48–55°C), which melts all the crystals in the chocolate. Add the remaining one-third of the chocolate, very finely chopped; this causes the chocolate to solidify. Finally, return the chocolate to the still warm bain-marie and allow it to melt again using the residual heat.

The exact temperatures for tempering will vary, depending on the type of chocolate you are using. Milk and white chocolates, for example, need lower temperatures, while bittersweet (dark) chocolate, with a high percentage of cocoa butter, needs a higher temperature. Couverture chocolate, used by many professionals, should have the recommended temperatures on the wrapping. If you use tempered chocolate for moulding Easter eggs and other shapes, you should achieve predictable results, and the unmoulding should be simple. For a really glossy finish, start with perfectly clean, dry moulds. Pour in the tempered chocolate, invert the mould over a wire rack to drain off any excess (there should be a layer about .5 cm/¼ in thick), then turn back into the upright position.

Leave the chocolate in the mould for about 24 hours in a cool room. To unmould, invert the mould and tap the back with a wooden spoon, then lift off.

At the risk of repeating myself, never let chocolate come into contact with direct heat or water. Both of these will cause melted chocolate to be ruined and it will have to be thrown away. Too much heat will burn the chocolate, and moisture will cause the chocolate to solidify.

A note on the recipe measurements:
    1 cup = 8 oz American cup
    1 pint = 20 oz Imperial pint
    1 tablespoon = 15 ml spoon
    1 teaspoon = 5 ml spoon
In England, single cream contains 18% fat, whipping cream 38·9%, and double cream 47·5% fat. If in doubt about which type to use, check the details on the container.

## PETITS POTS À LA BERGAMOTE

This is the simplest and most delicious chocolate pudding recipe I know. The scalded cream cooks the chocolate, and the tea adds a delicate perfume. The texture is sublime, and forms the basis of the "ganache".

### Serves 6

*4 oz (125 g) best-quality bittersweet (dark) chocolate, such as Valrhona Guanaja, preferably with 70% cocoa solids\**
*1½ cups (12 fl oz/350 ml) light (single) cream*
*1 tbsp of bergamot-flavoured tea leaves, such as Earl Grey or Pelham Mixture*
*1 tsp orange-flower water*

Finely chop the chocolate and put it into a heatproof bowl.

Boil the cream with the tea leaves for about 1 minute. Strain the cream into a jug, then stir in the orange-flower water. Slowly pour the hot, flavoured cream over the chocolate, stirring with a spatula, until smooth. Pour into small coffee cups or ramekins and chill for at least 2 hours.

\*If less concentrated chocolate is used, increase the quantity to 6 oz (175 g).

## LUCY TATE'S
## DEVIL'S FOOD CAKE

One of my oldest recipes, this was given to me by my best friend at school when we were about 10 years old. It is always most delicious when eaten in the middle of the night with a glass of very cold milk, as part of an illicit feast.

**Serves 8**
*5-6 oz (150-175 g) best-quality bittersweet (dark)*
*chocolate, broken into pieces*
*1 cup (8 fl oz/250 ml) milk*
*1 cup (8 oz/250 g) sugar*
*2 eggs, separated*
*2¼ cups (9 oz/275 g) all-purpose (plain) flour*
*2½ tsp baking powder*
*¼ tsp salt*
*½ cup (4 oz/125 g) butter, softened*
*1 tsp pure vanilla extract (essence)*

*For the frosting (icing)*
*scant ½ cup (3½ oz/100 g) sugar*
*1 tbsp golden syrup or honey*
*4 oz (125 g) bittersweet (dark) chocolate, melted*
*2 tbsp (1 oz/25 g) butter*
*1 tsp pure vanilla extract (essence)*

In a saucepan over low heat, melt together the chocolate, 6 tbsp of the milk and ½ cup plus 2 tbsp (4 oz/125 g) of the sugar. Stir over a low heat, then mix in 2 egg yolks and continue stirring until the mixture is smooth. Remove from the heat and leave to cool. Meanwhile, grease an 8 in/20 cm cake pan. Preheat the oven to 350°F (180°C, Gas 4).

Sift together the flour, baking powder and salt. In another bowl, cream together the butter with the remaining sugar. Add the vanilla to the remaining milk.

Fold the flour mixture into the creamed butter and sugar alternately with the vanilla-flavoured milk, then stir in the cooled chocolate mixture. If the mixture seems too dry, add a little more milk. Beat the egg whites until stiff peaks form, then fold them into the batter.

Pour the batter into the prepared cake pan and bake until the top of the cake springs back when lightly pressed, about 45 minutes. Cool on a wire rack.

Meanwhile, prepare the frosting (icing). Melt the sugar and golden syrup or honey with 6 tbsp water, then cover the pan and bring to a boil. Use a candy (sugar) thermometer and boil until the mixture reaches 225°F (110°C), or the soft ball stage. Take care not to overboil or the mixture will become brittle. Leave to cool to lukewarm, without stirring, then stir in the melted chocolate, butter and vanilla. Stir until the mixture reaches a good spreading consistency. This makes enough frosting to cover the top and sides of an 8 in/20 cm cake, so double the quantities if you want to make a layer cake.

## CHOCOLAT À L'ANCIENNE

The secret recipe of Rosa Cannabich, a contemporary of
Mozart. This is a wonderfully unctuous drink, which I tasted
recently. It was served to the "Court" audience in the inner
sanctum during a performance called "Mozart au chocolat" by
a troupe of French performers when they came to London.
Mozart himself is reputed to have tasted this at Mannheim in
1778.

### Serves 4
*6 oz (160 g) best-quality bittersweet (dark) chocolate,*
*preferably with 61% cocoa solids*
*small pinch of salt*
*2¼ cups (18 fl oz/500 ml) milk*
*1 tbsp superfine (caster) sugar*
*2 tbsp glass dark rum*
*1 demi-tasse cup (2 fl oz/50 ml) espresso coffee*

For the whipped cream
*¼ cup (2 fl oz/50 ml) crème fraîche or heavy (double) cream*
*2 tbsp milk*
*1½ tsp superfine (caster) sugar*

For the grated chocolate
*¾ oz (20 g) high-quality bittersweet (dark) chocolate*

Make the whipped cream in advance. Chill the bowl in which
you are going to whip the crème fraîche. Add the crème
fraîche, milk and sugar. Beat with an electric hand-held
beater, until stiff, but do not over beat or it will turn to butter.
Chill until you are ready to serve the chocolate.

Finely chop the chocolate and place in a saucepan with the salt and ¼ cup (2 fl oz/50 ml) water. Melt over a low heat, stirring constantly and taking great care that it does not burn, or the flavour will be ruined.

When the chocolate is smooth and shiny, stir in the milk and then the sugar. Bring to a boil, then simmer for 5 minutes. Be very careful because the chocolate bubbles up and thickens rapidly. Stir in the rum and coffee and boil 2 minutes longer. Beat the chocolate with a whisk to lighten it. When ready to

serve, add a spoonful of the whipped crème fraîche to each portion of hot chocolate and top with grated chocolate.

In summer, this is delicious served chilled. Leave the chocolate to cool, then stir in some crushed ice. When it has melted, serve the chocolate with the whipped crème fraîche and grated chocolate.

To make the grated chocolate, put the chocolate in the freezer for 2 hours to harden. Grate with a sharp knife or a potato peeler. Although this recipe seems to break all the cardinal rules about heating chocolate and adding liquid, it does work, and is almost a meal in itself!

## MOLE POBLANO

Legend maintains that this classic Mexican recipe was invented by the nuns of Puebla, near Mexico City, for their bishop, hence the name, which means literally 'of the village'. Although the idea of turkey in chocolate sauce is anathema to most people, it is a really rich, spicy and savoury sauce, not unlike an Indian korma sauce, made with almonds and spices. I like to serve this dish with a mixture of brown rice and wild rice. This version of the recipe is from Patricia Namm, one of the most enthusiastic members of The Chocolate Society.

Serves 4
sesame oil for frying
4 ancho chillies
3 pasilla chillies
1 lb (500 g) skinless turkey or chicken scallops (escallops)
1 quart (1¾ pints/950 ml) vegetable or chicken stock
⅓ cup (2 oz/50 g) sesame seeds, plus extra for garnishing
sea salt
2 tbsp pumpkin seeds
1 onion, grated
1 tbsp sesame oil
1 whole 5-star anise
½ tsp freshly ground cinnamon
¼ cup (1 oz/25 g) best-quality cocoa powder
1½ cups (12 oz/350 g) tomato puree (passata), or 2½ cups
(1 lb/500 g) peeled, seeded and chopped tomatoes
2 tsp brown rice syrup
5 whole black peppercorns

Lightly coat the inside of a skillet (frying pan) with sesame oil and fry both types of chillies for 2 minutes, shaking the pan and stirring occasionally so the chillies do not burn. Remove the chillies from the pan and soak them in a bowl of cold water for 30 minutes.

Gently poach the turkey or chicken scallops in the stock until just cooked through and slightly firm. Transfer to a glass or enamel dish and cover. Strain the stock into a jug and save for using in the sauce.

Toast the sesame seeds in a dry skillet with a pinch of sea salt until they are aromatic and begin to pop. Grind $\frac{1}{3}$ cup (2 oz/50 g) of the sesame seeds in a food processor or blender, reserving the remainder for a garnish. Toast the pumpkin seeds in the same dry skillet.

Combine the sesame and pumpkin seeds with the onion in an enamel saucepan with the sesame oil. Gently sauté for a few minutes, until the onion softens.

Remove the chillies from the bowl, discarding the soaking liquid. Remove the chillies' stems and seeds, then add them whole to the onion mixture with the 5-star anise, cinnamon, cocoa powder, passata or tomatoes, rice syrup, peppercorns and sea salt to taste. Simmer, uncovered, 20 minutes, adding more stock from the jug if necessary to thin, but the consistency should be quite thick, like satay sauce.

Remove from heat and leave the sauce to cool. Press through a sieve. Pour several tablespoons of the sauce around and over the scallops and leave to stand for at least 1 hour so they absorb the flavour.

To serve, gently reheat the scallops. Heat the remaining sauce and serve it separately. If necessary, thin with a little of the reserved stock. Garnish with extra toasted sesame seeds.

NOTE: For a more fiery, smoky flavour, add 2 or more chipotle peppers to the sauce while it cooks. These chillies are traditionally eaten in Mexico during Lent and are available in cans. They should have their seeds and stems removed before adding to the sauce.

## CHOCOLATE TRUFFLES

Coating these truffles in tempered chocolate gives them a crisp shell, which is a wonderful contrast to the soft centre.

Do not use a whisk for mixing the chocolate and cream together if you want to keep these truffles for a week or more, because any air pockets will encourage the growth of mould. These truffles can be frozen, but the container needs to be wrapped carefully in plastic wrap (cling film) and brought back to room temperature slowly to avoid condensation forming.

**Makes about 50**

⅔ cup (5 fl oz/150 ml) light (single) cream
10 oz (300 g) best-quality bittersweet (dark) chocolate
ideally with over 60% cocoa solids, chopped
¼ cup (2 fl oz/50 ml) 45% light or dark rum, or any other
alcohol or fruit liqueur you might prefer
2 tbsp unsalted butter, softened
8 oz (250 g) best-quality bittersweet (dark) chocolate,
tempered (page 93)
1 cup (4 oz/100 g) dusting powder made by sifting equal
amounts of cocoa powder and confectioners' (icing)
sugar together

Bring the cream to a boil. Put the chocolate in a heatproof bowl, then pour on the cream in a slow, steady stream and beat as if making mayonnaise. If any of the chocolate does not melt, put the bowl in a bain marie to warm gently. It is important to ensure that the ganache is smooth and shiny without lumps.

Beat in the butter, then add the rum slowly, little by little. Chill in the refrigerator about 10 minutes, until the ganache is thickened but not hard. If it becomes hard, you will have to melt it again. Put the ganache in a bowl and melt for a few

seconds in a bain marie to dissipate the skin which will have formed, stirring slowly. The mixture should now look like soft buttercream frosting (icing).

Put the ganache mixture into a pastry (piping) bag fitted with a plain nozzle and pipe into kisses on a tray lined with waxed (greaseproof) paper. Make each truffle a bit smaller than a walnut, about ¾ in (2 cm) but not too small or it will be lost.

Refrigerate until cool, then dip into the tempered chocolate using two forks and then into the dusting powder. Shake off any surplus dusting powder in a sieve.

# TARTE PUR CARAIBE

This recipe is from Frederic Bau, premier Chef Patissier and superstar of Valrhona, the fine chocolate makers who created this delicious dessert. These quantities can be halved, but as it is such a performance to make this and the recipe uses so much chocolate, it is worth doing on a large scale for a grand party. It is a sensationally rich and delicious dessert.

### Makes 4 tarts for 6 people

For the shortbread base
1/2 cup (4 oz/125 g) butter, softened
pinch of salt
1/2 cup (2 oz/50 g) confectioners' (icing) sugar, sifted
2 tbsp finely ground blanched almonds
1 egg
2 cups (8 oz/225 g) all-purpose (plain) flour

For the chocolate sponge
6 oz (175 g) best-quality couverture chocolate, such as Pur
Caraibe, preferably with over 60% cocoa solids
6 tbsp (3 oz/75 g) butter
6 egg whites
1/4 cup (2 oz/50 g) sugar
4 egg yolks

For the chocolate ganache
2 1/2 cups (1 pint/600 ml) heavy (whipping) cream
18 oz/500 g best-quality bittersweet (dark) chocolate, such
as Pur Caraibe, chopped
1 3/4 sticks (7 oz/200 g) butter, softened

2 oz/50 g melted chocolate, to paint the shortbread base

edible gold or silver leaf, to decorate


Make the shortbread base dough the day before baking. Cream together the butter with the salt, confectioners' (icing) sugar and ground almonds. Beat in the egg and 1/2 cup (2 oz/50 g) of the flour. When the paste is smooth, quickly work in the remaining flour. Shape into a ball, wrap in plastic wrap (cling film) and leave overnight in a cool place.

The next day, preheat the oven to 425°F (220°C/Gas 7). Thinly roll out the pastry dough and use to line four 8 in/20 cm buttered and floured tart pans with removable bases, each 1 in/2 cm deep. Take care not to stretch the pastry, or it will shrink away from the sides during baking. Prick the bases well, then bake for 10-15 minutes, until lightly coloured and completely baked. Cool on a wire rack.

To make the chocolate sponge, preheat the oven to 350°F (180°C/Gas 4). Melt the chocolate and butter at 113°F (45°C). Beat the egg whites and sugar together. Using a whisk, add the egg yolks, then fold in the melted chocolate and butter. Pour the batter into 2 lightly greased and floured 7 in/18 cm cake pans (tins) and bake for about 10 minutes. Cool on a wire rack. When cool, trim the top and cut into 2 perfectly flat discs of cake.

To make the ganache, bring the heavy (whipping) cream to a boil. Slowly pour it on to the chocolate, stirring constantly, as if making mayonnaise. When the ganache is smooth and no hotter than 100°F (40°C) add the butter and stir well. The temperature of the ganache is critical because if it is too hot the butter will melt and sink to the bottom, making the mixture very heavy.

To assemble the tarts, when the shortbread bases are at room temperature, "paint" the tops with the couverture chocolate and place the trimmed sponge cakes on top at once. Pour over the liquid ganache, then chill 1-2 hours in the refrigerator or a cool pantry (larder) until the ganache sets. If the ganache is not perfectly flat and even, leave in a warm place (the bottom of a cool oven will do) for 1-2 minutes so it melts and levels off.

When finally cool, decorate each tart with a little edible gold or silver leaf (available from Asian grocers), cut into star or moon shapes or just sprinkled over the tops.

# LADY ELINOR FETTISPLACE'S
# CHOCOLATE CREAMS

This Elizabethan dessert could well be England's earliest chocolate recipe. This version comes from Hilary Spurling's book *Lady Elinor Fettisplace's Elizabethan Recipe Book*.

*To make chocolate cream*
*Take a Quart of cream, 3 ounces of Chocolate grated,*
*boyle it well together & let it stand till tis cold, & yn put ye*
*whites of 6 Eggs beaten to a Froth & sweeten it to your Taste,*
*& then mill it up.*

Chocolate from the New World began to be sold in England in the 1650s: the first London chocolate house was opened in 1657; White's Club in St James' started life as another shortly afterwards, by which time chocolate was well on the way to becoming an exceedingly fashionable drink. This mixture makes one of those semi-solid confections like a syllabub, part dessert, part thick, frothy drink:

For 6 generous glassfuls, scald 2½ cups (1 pint/600 ml) of light (single) cream by bringing it to a boil, then coarsely grate in 2 or 3 oz (50 or 75 g) of the best-quality bittersweet (dark) chocolate (this is double the amount specified above, but the cocoa butter in natural cocoa beans made 17th-century chocolate richer than ours), and simmer the mixture gently for a few minutes. When it is quite cold, beat 3 egg whites until they stand in peaks, with a heaped tablespoon of sugar (more if you like a sweeter taste), and fold in the chocolate cream. Beat it well: "mill it up" meant whipping the mixture with a specially designed, notched wooden chocolate beater or mill which has been used for centuries*.

Pour the cream into glasses, leave it to set in the refrigerator, and serve with more grated chocolate on the top. It should develop a stiff foam, or head, so much liked in the seventeenth and eighteenth centuries, with a runnier chocolate underneath – less cloying than chocolate mousse, frothier and more ethereal than a cold soufflé set with gelatine.
*Molinillo* – a Mexican invention, widely used in the preparation of drinking chocolate.

## WIDGEON AU CHOCOLAT

From Massialot's *Cuisinier roïal et bourgoise* (1691). Is this recipe for a wild duck in a ragout with chocolate the earliest French recipe? It certainly may be the only published Aztec recipe in seventeenth-century France using chocolate as a thickener.

*Having plucked and cleaned your widgeon, eviscerate it and wash it. Scald it and put it in a pot and season it with salt, pepper, bayleaf, and a bouquet garni; you make a little chocolate which you throw in. Prepare at the same time a ragoût, with the livers, mushroom, morels, truffles and a quarteron of chestnuts. When your widgeon is cooked and arranged on its dish, you pour your ragoût over it, and serve garnished with whatever you wish.*

## MARBLED CHOCOLATE BRIOCHE

Like most yeast recipes this is not as time consuming as it sounds, especially as other tasks can be done while the dough is rising. This is an attractive-looking brioche, and the chocolate lumps can be divided between the chocolate and plain doughs, or put only in the chocolate one for a more dramatic effect.

### Serves 10-12
*1 tsp active dry yeast (dried yeast)*
*2 tbsp milk, warm*
*scant 3 cups (12 oz/350 g) white bread flour*
*pinch of salt*
*¼ cup (2 oz/50 g) sugar*
*½ cup (2 oz/50 g) best-quality cocoa powder*
*3 eggs, lightly beaten*
*½ cup plus 2 tbsp (5 oz/150 g) butter, softened*
*1 oz (25 g) best-quality bittersweet (dark) chocolate, chopped into small lumps*

Dissolve the yeast in the milk and set aside until it starts to bubble and froth. Sift the flour into a large bowl, then stir in the salt and sugar. Divide the flour into two portions of 1¼ cups (5 oz/150 g) and 1¾ cups (7 oz/200 g). Place each portion into separate bowls and sift the cocoa powder into the smaller portion.

Pour half the yeast mixture into each of the bowls of flour. Likewise add half the eggs and butter to each portion.

Beat the ingredients in both bowls until well combined. Leave the bowls in a warm place for the doughs to rise, about 2 hours, until doubled in size.

When the doughs are bubbly and spongy, break them down with a wooden spoon. Put both doughs in separate clean, greased bowls, cover with plastic wrap (cling film) and leave overnight in a cool place.

In the morning, butter a 10 in/25 cm kugglehopf or brioche mould. Break down both doughs and knead briefly for about 30 seconds, until the air has been pushed out. Add the chocolate pieces to both or one portion.

Place 1 tablespoon of white dough in the mould, then add 1 tablespoon chocolate dough, alternating the 2 doughs until both are used. The dough should come half way up the sides of the mould. Cover with plastic wrap (cling film) and leave in a warm place until the dough rises to the top of the mould, about 1 hour.

Meanwhile, preheat the oven to 375°F (190°C, Gas 5). Bake 20 to 25 minutes, or until the brioche sounds hollow when tapped on the bottom. Turn out and cool on a wire rack.

## MADAME DUMOUCHEL'S CLASSIC FRENCH CHOCOLATE MOUSSE

A simple, soft chocolate mousse.

**Serves 8**
*8 oz (250 g) best-quality bittersweet (dark) chocolate*
*1/2 cup (2 oz/50 g) unsalted butter, softened*
*9 egg whites*
*1/2 cup (4 oz/125 g) superfine (caster) sugar*
*6 egg yolks*

Slowly melt the chocolate. Beat with the butter in a large bowl.

Using an electric mixer, whisk the egg whites until frothy. Add 1 tbsp of the sugar and continue beating on low. When the sugar dissolves, increase the speed to the maximum. When the egg whites are stiff, shake the remaining sugar gently onto them; if it is added too quickly it will liquify the egg whites. Beat the meringue to make it strong and elastic, then mix in the egg yolks.

Stir half the meringue mixture into the chocolate and butter mixture. Fold in the remaining meringue mixture with a large wooden spoon, working from the outside to the middle. Work calmly and slowly. There is no need to worry about the mousse setting because the butter keeps it soft. Pour into 1 large soufflé dish or individual ones and refrigerate.

## PEAR AND CHOCOLATE TART

The golden colour of the cape gooseberries make a beautiful contrast to the dark chocolate tart in this recipe.

**Serves 8**

For the pastry
*heaped 1½ cups (7 oz/200 g) all-purpose (plain) flour*
*5 tbsp cocoa powder*
*½ cup plus 2 tbsp (5 oz/150 g) butter,*
*well chilled and diced*
*2 tbsp superfine (caster) sugar*
*pinch of salt*
*1 egg, beaten*

For the filling
*1¼ cups (½ pint/300 ml) heavy (whipping) cream*
*5 oz (150 g) best-quality bittersweet (dark) chocolate with*
*more than 60% cocoa solids, finely chopped*
*3 ripe pears, peeled and quartered*
*confectioners' (icing) sugar and 3 cape gooseberries,*
*to decorate*

To make the pastry, sift the flour, cocoa powder, sugar and salt into a bowl. Cut in (rub in) the butter until the mixture resembles breadcrumbs. Add enough of the egg to bind the dough, then gather together into a ball and wrap in plastic wrap (cling film). Chill for at least 30 minutes.

Meanwhile, preheat the oven to 425°F (220°C, Gas 7). Roll out the dough and use it to line a 10 in/25 cm tart pan with a removable bottom. Line the dough with foil and dry beans and bake for 10 minutes. Remove the foil and beans, lower the temperature to 325°F (160°C, Gas 3) and bake for about 5 minutes longer, until the pastry is dry in the centre. Do not turn off the oven.

To make the filling, bring the cream to a boil, then pour over the chocolate and stir to make a ganache. Place the pear quarters on the pastry case and pour the ganache over them. Return to the oven for 20 minutes, until the filling begins to set. Remove from the oven and place on a wire rack to cool.

# CLAUDIA RODEN'S
# CHOCOLATE CAKE

Claudia says this recipe is Sephardic. The original version included melted butter, but she and I both prefer this version without it. Easy to make, this delicious cake is not overly rich, and is a favourite with all the family and the party piece of Simon Roden, my brother-in-law.

**Serves 12**

*8 oz (250 g) best-quality bittersweet or semisweet (dark)*
*chocolate*
*2 tbsp milk*
*4 oz (125 g) finely ground blanched almonds*
*¾ cup (6 oz/175 g) sugar*
*6 eggs, separated*
*superfine (caster) sugar for decoration*
*butter and cake flour for the cake pan*

Preheat the oven to 350°F (180°C/Gas 4). Lightly butter and flour a 10 in/25 cm springform cake pan with a removable base.

Melt the chocolate with the milk in the top of a bain-marie. Mix together with the ground almonds, sugar and egg yolks and beat well. Beat the egg whites until stiff, then fold into the chocolate mixture.

Pour the batter into the cake pan and bake 45 minutes to 1 hour, depending on whether a drier or moister cake is preferred. Cool in the pan. Remove the sides of the pan and serve the cake on the base. Sprinkle with superfine (caster) sugar.

## CHOCOLATE FONDUE GUANAJA

A guest-participation dessert on the lines of a Swiss fondue. Place the fondue pot over its burner or a bowl on the table over a night-light stand or an electric warmer and let guests prepare their own dessert. The fondue mixture can be prepared in advance but it must be reheated very slowly to soften it just before serving.

**Serves 6–8**

*¾ cup (6 fl oz/175 ml) heavy (whipping) cream*
*2 tbsp milk*
*7 oz (200 g) best-quality couverture chocolate, such as*
*Guanaja, finely chopped*
*fruit and bread, chopped*

Bring the cream and milk to a boil, then pour over the chocolate in a heatproof bowl. Stir slowly for 2 to 3 minutes, until the chocolate melts.

Simply dunk pieces of fresh pineapple, pear, nuts or brioche into the mixture.

## WHITE CHOCOLATE ICE CREAM
## WITH POPPY SEEDS

This recipe is from Sue
Clapperton, Chef Patissier at
the Royal Oak Hotel,
Sevenoaks, England. Try it
with Glace Caraibe (page
.114) for an interesting
combination.

**Serves 6**
*1 vanilla bean (pod)*
*1¼ cups (10 fl oz/300 ml) whole milk, or*
*half milk and half light (single) cream*
*1 large egg*
*1 extra egg yolk*
*2 tbsp sugar*
*3½ oz/100 g best-quality white chocolate, chopped*
*1 tbsp black poppy seeds*

To make the custard base, place the vanilla bean (pod) in the
milk, or milk and cream, and bring to a boil. Leave to infuse
for 20 minutes.

Beat the whole egg, the extra yolk and the sugar together,
then slowly beat in the warm vanilla-flavoured milk, beating
constantly with a balloon whisk. Return the mixture to the
rinsed-out pan, or a bain-marie, and heat, stirring constantly,
until the custard thickens and coats the back of a spoon. Be
careful not to let the mixture overheat or you will have
scrambled egg.

Gradually pour the hot custard over the chopped white
chocolate, stirring constantly, until the chocolate melts. Stir in
the poppy seeds. Churn in an ice-cream maker for 20-25
minutes, or according to the manufacturer's directions. Check
for consistency and serve at once or place in the freezer.

# THE CHOCOLATE SOCIETY'S
# GLACE CARAIBE

This wonderfully rich chocolate ice cream is best made with
Valrhona Caraibe couverture blended with whipped cream. If
this brand is unavailable, use another quality couverture. It is
particularly good topped with finely chopped hazelnuts or
almonds. For a really dramatic effect, serve in Chocolate
Baskets (page 115), along with White Chocolate Ice Cream
with Poppy Seeds (page 113).

**Serves 10**
*1¼ cups (10 fl oz/300 ml) light (single) cream*
*4 oz/125 g best-quality couverture chocolate, ideally*
*Valrhona Caraibe, finely chopped*
*4 egg yolks*
*½ cup (3½ oz/100 g) superfine (caster) sugar*
*⅔-1¼ cups (5-10 fl oz/150-300 ml) heavy (double) cream,*
*added to taste*

Scald the light (single) cream, then remove from the heat and
add the chocolate. Leave to melt, then stir gently until smooth.

Beat the egg yolks with the sugar until pale and thick, then
slowly beat in the chocolate and cream mixture. Put this
mixture in a bain-marie and return to the heat, stirring
constantly until the custard thickens and coats the back of the
spoon.

Whip the heavy (double) cream until thick, but not too stiff.
Pour the chocolate custard into a large bowl. Fold in the
whipped cream to taste.

Pour into a freezerproof container or serving dish and freeze
until solid.

## CHOCOLATE BASKETS

Ideal for a dramatic serving of ice cream, sorbet or simply an array of bright-red summer fruits.

**Makes 4**

*8 oz/250 g best-quality Couverture chocolate, melted*
*(see page 93)*

For each basket, cut out a double thickness 6 in/15 cm square of aluminium foil. Wrap the foil tightly around a small orange, leaving the edges loose to give the basket shape. Remove the orange and press the foil down on a firm surface to make a flat base.

Spoon all but 2 tbsp of the chocolate into the foil cases, smoothing it up the sides with the back of a spoon. Place the reserve chocolate into a pastry (piping) bag and pipe a lacy chocolate edge on each basket.

Chill or freeze until firmly set. Peel away the foil gently, starting at the top and working down to the base.

## MANJARI CHOCOLATE SAUCE

A very simple but delicious chocolate sauce. This recipe's success depends on both the quality of the chocolate used and the method of making an emulsion with the chocolate and liquids. As always with chocolate, never put the chocolate into the pan with hot liquid, or in contact with direct heat, as the chocolate will be ruined in both instances.

This chocolate will keep for a day or two in the refrigerator but it will have to be reheated in a bain marie.

**Makes about 3 cups (1¾ pints/750 ml)**
*8 oz/250 g best-quality bittersweet (dark) chocolate, ideally Valrhona's Manjari 64% pure criollo bean chocolate*
*½ cup (4 fl oz/125 ml) whipping cream*
*½ cup (4 fl oz/125 ml) milk*

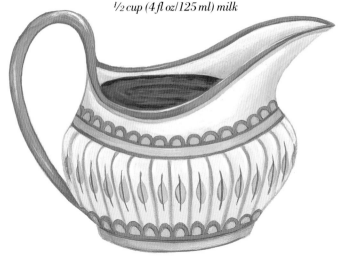

Chop the chocolate as finely as possible; the pieces should not be any larger than peas. Place in a heatproof bowl.

Bring the cream and milk to a boil. Add the hot liquid little by little to the chocolate, beating constantly to make an emulsion, as if making mayonnaise. Serve immediately.

## CROSTINI WITH GOAT'S CHEESE AND CHOCOLATE TAPENADE

This recipe is a variation of Claudia Roden's olive toasts. The chocolate and goats' cheese add an interesting twist. The chocolate should be hardly discernible, but when explained should give guests food for thought.

### Makes about 30 pieces

*1 oz/25 g best-quality bittersweet (dark) chocolate, melted*
*1 cup (5 oz/150 g) pitted ripe (black) olives*
*4 canned anchovy fillets, well drained and chopped*
*1 large clove garlic, chopped*
*2 tbsp capers, the vinegar squeezed out*
*5 tbsp good-quality olive oil, plus a little extra for covering mixture*
*French or Italian bread for serving*
*8 oz/250 g goats' cheese*
*cayenne pepper for sprinkling*

Optional Ingredients
*2 tbsp rum*
*some fine chopped fresh chilli*
*a few sprigs fresh parsley or dill*

Put all the ingredients, including the rum, if you are using, but not the goats' cheese, cayenne pepper and fresh herbs, in the food processor and quickly blend so the first five ingredients are just blended but not turned into a paste.

Press the mixture into a little pot. Cover with a thin layer of oil if you wish to keep this tapenade long.

To prepare the toast, cut some French or Italian bread into thin slices and bake in a 350°F (180°C/Gas 4) oven until crisp. Cool the toast on a wire rack. Spread with the tapenade, and place thin slices of goats' cheese on top. Sprinkle with cayenne pepper and add the fresh herbs only when you are about to serve.

## UK SUPPLIERS

### Retail Outlets

Bentalls, Anstee House, Wood Street, Kingston, Surrey KT1 1TX (081) 541 6924

Big Rock Candy Mountain, 100–102, Galleria, Comet Way, Hatfield, Herts AL10 9TF (0707) 251590

Broughton Crafts, High Street, Stockbridge, Hampshire SO20 6HB (0264) 810513

The Candy Box, 32a, High Street, Grantown on Spey, Moray PH26 3EG (0479) 3498

Cannelle Ltd, 705 Tudor Estate, Abbey Road, London NW10 7UW (081) 453 0090

Chocs Away, 48, High Street, Honiton, Devon EX14 8PQ (0404) 45968

Cotswold Chocolate Company, The Brambles, Theescombe Lane, Amberley, Glos GL5 5AZ (0453) 873557

Cullens, 112/114 Holland Park Avenue, London W11 4VA (071) 221 7139

Delights of Carlisle, 28 Fisher Street, Carlisle, Cumbria CA4 8RF (0228) 818709

Fitzbillies, Trumpington Street, Cambridge (0223) 352500

Garden Store, 32, Museum Street, Holborn, London WC1 (071) 637 4309

Harrods, Knightsbridge, London SW1X 7XL (071) 730 1234

Heals and Son Ltd, 196, Tottenham Court Road, London W1P 9LD (071) 636 1666

Helens Choc Shop, Ash Street, Bowness on Windermere, Cumbria (0539) 446869

Howells of Cardiff, 14, St Mary's Street, Cardiff CF1 1TT (0222) 231055

Kendals, Deangate, Manchester M60 3AV (061) 832 3414

Lewis Oxford, 27 Westgate, Oxford OX1 1LP

Mackintosh of Marlborough, 42a, High Street, Marlborough, Wiltshire SN9 5OZ (0672) 514069

Rackhams of Birmingham Ltd, Corporation Street, Birmingham (021) 236 3333

Rococo, 321 Kings Road, London SW3 5EP (071) 352 5857

Selfridges Ltd, 400, Oxford Street, London W1E 3WB (071) 029 1234

Theobroma, 91, West Yard, Camden Lock Place, Chalk Farm Road, London NW1 8AF (071) 284 2670

Valvona and Crolla, 19, Elm Row, Edinburgh EH7 4AA

Vivians, 2 Worpel Way, Richmond, Surrey TW10 6DF (081) 940 3600

For further information, please contact The Chocolate Society of Great Britain, Norwood Bottom Farm, Otley, Leeds, West Yorkshire LS21 2RA (0943) 851101

## US SUPPLIERS

### Wholesale Outlets

Dairyland, New York (212) 842 8700

European Imports, Chicago (312) 226 8060

Gourm-e-co, Washington (703) 430 5616

Made in France, San Francisco (415) 822 3438

Optimus, Miami (800) 722 8427

Van Rex, Los Angeles (213) 965 1320

Harry Wils, New York (212) 431 9731

### Retail Outlets

Balduccis, 424 Avenue of the Americas, New York

Bloomingdales, 69th Street, New York

Dean & DeLuca, 652 Broadway, New York

Macys, Union Square, San Francisco
Sacks, 5th Avenue, New York
Williams-Sonoma stores in the
following locations:
Alexandria, Atlanta, Austin, Bal
Harbor, Baltimore, Beachwood,
Beverly Hills, Boca Raton, Boston,
Brea, Bridgewater,
Buffalo, Burlingame, Burlington,
Chestnut Hill, Chicago, Cincinnati,
Cleveland, Corte Madera,
Columbus, Costa Mesa, Cranston,
Cupertino, Dallas, Denver, Fairfax,
Farmington, Ft Lauderdale,

Germantown, Glen Burnie,
Houston, Indianapolis, Kansas City,
Kensington, Lake Forest, Livonia,
Manchasset, McLean, Minneapolis,
Nashville, New York City,
Oakbrook, Oklahoma City, Owings
Mill, Palm Beach, Palo Alto,
Pasadena, Phoenix, Plantation,
Portland, Princeton, Reston,
Ridgewood, Rolling Hills Estates,
Sacramento, St Louis, Schaumburg,
San Antonio, San Diego, Santa Ana,
Santa Barbara, Troy, Tulsa, Walnut
Creek, Washington, DC, Woodland
Hills

## BIBLIOGRAPHY

*Cambridge History of Latin America*, Ed. Leslie Bethel, Cambridge University Press
Colmenero, Antonio, *A Curious Treatise of the Nature and Quality of Chocolate*, J. Okes, 1640
De Blegny, Nicholas, *Le Bon Usage de Thé, Caffé, et du Chocolat*, Paris, 1687
Drummond, J. C. & Wilbraham A., *The Englishman's Food*, Jonathan Cape, 1939
Dufour, Sylvestre, *Making Coffee, Tea, Chocolate*, 1685
Franklin, Alfred, *La Vie Privée d'Autrefois*, E. Plon Nourrit et Cie, 1893
Gage, Thomas, *A New Survey of the West Indies*, 1648
Historicus, *Cocoa All About It*, Sampsom Low, London, 1903
Masson, Pierre, *Le Parfait Limonadier*, Charles Moette, 1705
Pelissier, Leon, *Lettres Inedites de la Comptesse d'Albany*, 1904
Prescott, W. H., *A Conquest of Mexico*, Chatto & Windus, 1922
Purefoy, *Letters*, Sidgwick & Jackson, 1931
Rubenstein, Helge, *The Chocolate Book*, Penguin
Scott-Thompson, Gladys, *Life in a Noble Household 1641–1700*, Jonathan Cape, 1937
Stubbe, Henry, *The Indian Nectar*, Andrew Crook, 1662
Walpole, Horace, *Letters*, Ed. W. S. Lewis
Wagner, Gillian, *A Chocolate Conscience*, Chatto and Windus, 1987
*Wynne Diaries, 1789–1920*, Oxford University Press, 1940

## ACKNOWLEDGEMENTS

I would like to thank all those people who have helped in the creation of this book. Firstly my mother, Sybil, who tirelessly researched the material; my husband, James, who went to China in order not to distract me; Darren and Sonja, who held the fort at Rococo; Alan and Nicola Porter, without whom The Chocolate Society would not exist; Thierry Dumouchel for his tireless explanations on the more complex aspects of chocolate tempering and moulding; Christophe Henry at Valrhona; Christina Smith who introduced me to Colin Webb of Pavilion Books, who commissioned the book; and finally to my editor, Rachel King, and everyone else at Pavilion who has been involved.

# INDEX

861   1824   1825   1826   1827   1828

110 Gr. 130

1829   1830   1831   1832   1833

180 Gr. 170

1834   1835   1836   1837   1838

868 bis   400 Gr. 210

1839   1840   1841   1842   1843

R CRÈME (DÉPOSÉS)

1844   1845   1846   1847   1848   1849

600 Gr. 260   PASTILLES POUR

557   558

Pesant environ 5 gram Le Moule par g .....5

562   563

MOULES ŒUFS A DESSINS RELIEF (Déposées)

2000   1999   1998

567   568

55 gr. 10ᵐ   40 gr. 9ᵐ   25 gr. 8ᵐ
La coquille 3ᶠ   La coquille 2ᶠ50   La coquille 2ᶠ25

2001   2002   2003

572   573

80 gr.   80 gr. 10ᵐ   100 gr. 12ᵐ
La coquille 3ᶠ50   La coquille 3ᶠ50   La coquille 4ᶠ

577   575

2004   2005   2006

Pesant environ 5g

125 gr. 13ᵐ   110 gr. 13ᵐ   100 gr. 12ᵐ
La coquille 4ᶠ   La coquille 3ᶠ50   La coquille 4ᶠ

CHOCOLAT

MOULES FANTAISIES

1445   1446